The Laidback Lifestyle

"ANYONE CAN HAVE IT"

The Laidback Approach to Achieving More, Stressing Less, and Living The Awesome Life You Deserve

ALAN MCCOMAS

*To my mom, Patsy Brown, for making
me who I am today.*

*And to my dad, Chuck McComas, who was never
around when I was growing up (which was probably
a good thing), but we did get to know each other
later in life and had some really good times together
before he passed away.*

TABLE OF CONTENTS

ACKNOWLEDGMENTS

I want to thank my wife Janie for supporting me during the writing of this book and encouraging me to keep going when it got frustrating. You are amazing, Janie, we are amazing together, and I love you. Our new favorite saying is "You have to go out on a limb because that's where the fruit is."

I want to thank Luke and Ashley for being the most outstanding people in the whole world. You guys make it so easy for me to be a dad. I love you both very much.

I also want to thank Chandler Bolt and the Self-Publishing School along with my personal book coach, Scott Allan. Without them this would definitely not have been possible. I've thought about writing this book for a while now but until I hooked up with Chandler and his group, nothing was going anywhere fast.

If you have thought about writing a book, I highly recommend going to these guys. Just use this link—it's that easy!

Use this link when checking out SPS

https://xe172.isrefer.com/go/sps4fta-vts/bookbrosinc1953

In addition I would like to thank my editor, Spencer Borup. He was fantastic. We were on the same page and he really understood what I wanted to say and how I wanted to say it.

And last but not least I would to thank my Core Launch Team, family and friends for keeping me moving forward and making sure I didn't do anything stupid.

Aaron Markel	Jack Anderson	Pat McComas
Ashley (McComas) Miller	Jackie Breheim	Kathy McComas
Barb Kody	Janie McComas	Mel Shelton
Bob Carpenter	Jason Miller	Matt Shanks
Chip Holcombe	Jason Smith	Rachel Griego
Chuck Breheim	Jason Sutermaster	Chris Griego
Carol Cook	Jason Vold	Rich Broderick
Dana Schultz	Jeff Matola	Rob Rankin
Darren Dicke	Jeri Rankin	Sara Ward
Dave Cook	Jim Hannon	Scott Allan
Debra Hendrickson	Jim Wisler	Shawn Ward
Dominika Perkowska	Jimmy Davis	Sherry Matola
Elaine Broderick	John Harman	Dr. John (Speedy) Boggess
Emily Degler	Joseph Dreher	Spencer Borup
Frances McCabe	Josh Bachus	Tim O'Neil
Frank Mamone	Julie Holcombe	TC Bradley
Greg Degler	Kelsey Schultz	Terry Deamron
Greg Justice	Kiera Sheets	Theresa Keller
Greg Keller	Luke McComas	Tony Crowe
Harry Yitsis	Lindsay McComas	Walter Heimbuch

INTRODUCTION

The *Laidback Lifestyle* is a simple, easy-to-read book that lays out basic principles on how to live with less stress, be more productive and achieve an abundance of happiness in all aspects of your life. It's all about the *attitude* and *mindset.*

There are many circumstances that are not in our control but we always have control over ourselves. Many people never have a laidback type of life. They live their entire life full of worry, trying to get ahead or just catch up and die without really enjoying the ride. We only get one ride. This is not what life should be about for anyone.

Even if you don't think that you're naturally a laidback person, this trait is very attainable regardless of your situation or personality. Whether it's not enough money, love, or happiness, anyone can improve their current situation with these basic tips on living your day-to-day life. This book outlines, in very simple terms, some of the basic steps and actions a person can take to improve their day-to-day life and enjoy it more. This is not a scientific reference book with a lot of facts and theories. This book breaks down and outlines some very basic, common-sense ways to improve your attitude, mindset and your overall outlook on life. And most importantly to do it with a sense of humor. You can read a whole chapter in just a few minutes each day and work at it one step at a time.

As all of us have done, I've had many failures and problems throughout my personal and business life. But I've never let any of these issues hold me down, at least for very long. In fact, I've plowed through adversity many times in my life and my attitude and mindset (the laidback style) has always pulled me through. You actually have to fail before you can succeed anyway.

The chapters in this book are to point out things to think about, and areas of your life to work on and improve. These philosophies are what got me where I am today. Some of these lessons of wisdom came along a lot later in life than I would have liked. But this is just a guide to get you thinking about what might be best for you to work on.

Everyone is naturally good at some things and not others. Think about what you have and don't have. Consider the qualities that you were born with and the ones you might want to improve upon. Some of these chapters might give you a lot to work on, and some might come naturally.

Reading this book may not be a "drastic overnight life-changing experience," but it can improve your life one little piece at a time. If you follow through with these tips on a regular basis I promise it will improve your lifestyle.

At the end of this book is a list of books, audios, websites and blogs to help you continue on your journey to having a laidback life.

So let's get this party started!

THE DEFINITION OF "LAIDBACK"

Before we begin, let's talk about the definition of the word "laidback." In fact, when you Google it, it's not a word at all. It comes up as two words: laid-back. But as far as I'm concerned, it's a word, and I'm going to use it as a word in this book. So get over it right now if you're an English teacher.

I'm sure everyone has their own definition of the word "laidback," and everyone *should* have their own definition. In fact, I encourage you to come up with your own definition.

The reason I use the word "laidback" so frequently is that it has been a part of my life for a long time. Back in 1987, I started a golf outing with a couple friends of mine, Tim O'Neil and Louie Curlee, called "The Laidback Golf Outing." At the time we did not realize how big this event would get. Along the way we added Harry Yitsis, Greg Justice and Wayne Pennington to The Laidback committee. The Laidback Golf Outing ran from 1987 until 2005.

Over a hundred people attended the golf outing year after year. And many of them from out of town flying in from all over the country. We would do it differently now for charity, but back then it was just a bunch of guys getting together to golf and party. Guys of all ages, occupations and backgrounds. But it didn't matter. Everybody became good friends and we just had a good time each year. A lot of people that became friends at those golf outings are still friends today, thirty years later, who would have never met otherwise. My point for bringing this up is when we first named it The Laidback, we didn't realize how spot-on we were with that name. It was just a laidback, casual outing that went on for almost twenty years, with all types of characters coming together as one big group. It was a great time every year and I'm very proud of what we created. The friendships, stories and memories from those golf outings are priceless.

In 1999, I bought a bar near my hometown of Ironton, Ohio. We remodeled the place and created a nice, casual bar where everyone could hang out. It was right on the Ohio River, on two and a half acres with a fantastic view of the sunset. I was thinking of naming it the Sunset Grill, referencing the great Eagles song. But my brother-in-law at the time, Pat Boggs, said that we had to call it "The Laidback." He said after all of these years having the The Laidback golf outing we couldn't call it anything else. Our goal (or mission statement) for the bar was the same concept as we accomplished in the golf outing. It was to bring a nice, casual venue to a lot of nice people that would meet, get along and just have a laidback time. So "The Laidback" it was. We owned it from 1999 to 2006. My brother-in-law ran the bar. I lived in Columbus two and a half hours away so only got down there every month or so. But the best part about that time of my life is that I got to reconnect with old friends from my hometown and made many more new friends at the same time. It wasn't about the bar; it was about connecting with my old and new hometown Ironton peeps. I love each and every one of them.

The reason I'm telling you about the golf outing and the bar is to explain how the word "laidback" has been a part of my life for a long time. Plus, the word goes hand-in-hand with all of my life philosophies and attitudes.

I have a lot of my own sayings and quotes that my friends call Al-isms. These are simple, funny, philosophical quotes and stories that I'll share in this book. And some of them are downright stupid. I am hooked on personal development and motivational books and tapes.

So about a year ago I decided to write a book to share my thoughts and tips on how anyone can have a laidback life, because I sure have. We'll get to those details and upcoming chapters but first I wanted to talk about the definition of "laidback."

If you Google "laidback," this is what you get:

laid-back
ˌl d'bak/
adjective
informal

1. relaxed and easygoing.
"a shaggy dog with an engaging, laid-back temperament"

synonyms:

> relaxed, easygoing, free and easy, casual, nonchalant, unexcitable, imperturbable, unruffled, blasé, cool, equable, even-tempered, no confrontational, low-

maintenance, insouciant, calm, unperturbed, unflustered, unflappable, unworried, unconcerned, unbothered; leisurely, unhurried, Type-B; stoical, phlegmatic, tolerant

That's a good definition and most of those words I would use in my own definition of "laidback" (easy going, casual, non-confrontational, low maintenance). They're all very good words. However, I want to add a few additional phrases to expand the definition that applies to this book. I am adding: work smarter not harder, be a servant, be a problem solver, contribute to others and use time wisely. Some of this might not make sense regarding the actual word laidback right now but they will later on in the book. The bottom line is to make life easier (not just for you but for everyone around you), minimize the stress in your life, maximize your productivity and enjoy life.

I am not referring to being nonchalant, lazy, nonproductive, or apathetic. In fact, I'm suggesting just the opposite. You can be laidback and still go a hundred and fifty miles an hour. This is about getting things done in the most efficient way possible and having more time to enjoy the things that you love. Keep things in perspective, be kind, and don't worry about anything that you don't have any control over. When you work and play in a laidback fashion, you will get more accomplished, in less time with less effort.

So now I have shared the Wikipedia definition of "laidback," I've explained my definition of "laidback" and I would like for you to come up with your own definition of the word "laidback." Everyone's definition will be different. Yours might be totally opposite from mine. You might want to sit on the beach all day, go fishing, and work less. There's no definition that is cast in stone so you can make it whatever you want. **Especially since it's not even a word.**

Write your own definition down and look at it every day. Put it on your screen saver, put it out in front of you, tape it on your wall. Do whatever you need to do but have it in front of you all the time and take a glance at it every day. I also recommend as you're going through this book to highlight certain chapters that resonate with you and identify specific areas that may require more of your attention than others.

In fact, now that I'm thinking about it more, you don't even have to use the word "laidback."

"Laidback" is the word that I use because of the golf outing, the bar, and it's just been part of my life for so long. You can use your own word that matches your personality. If you want to make up your own word go ahead. I did.

There are no specific rules to this laidback concept that I'm going to talk about in this book. Be your own person and use your own word. Don't complicate it and don't over think it. Keep it simple which is exactly what you will learn in the following chapters.

If you want to use the word "laidback," I'll give you permission. After all, I'm claiming the rights to it (if there is such a thing) so I can give anyone the right to use it if I want.

I'm no attorney, but I did stay in a Holiday Inn Express once.

THE BIG PICTURE
"JUST GET HIGH"

Now that I have your attention with the title of the chapter, I better clarify myself. No, I'm not talking about going in the basement and rolling a big fat joint or flying to Colorado to do some shopping at the local pot store.

I'm talking about taking a look at your life from a distance. In other words, take a look at the big picture before diving into the details. We'll get into the nitty-gritty details after this chapter, but let's evaluate the world and life from a distance at first to get some perspective on what really matters and what we have control over.

Sometimes it's just easier to see things from afar. It's like not being able to see the forest for the trees, that type of thing. You have to be able to see and appreciate the overall situation before breaking it down and fixing all the little pieces one at a time.

So let's take a look at the big picture and ask ourselves why we want a laidback life and why we don't think we have it now.

Did you see how I added "and why we think we don't have it now"? You could very possibly already have a laidback life and not realize it, or even worse, you don't appreciate it. If the latter part is the case, this book will help you realize and appreciate what you have. If not, then we'll work on getting you to that laidback status to start with, and then you can appreciate it in the future.

If you look at the Earth from way out in outer space, it is very small. Compared to the universe and beyond it is very, very, very small. In fact, it's a speck of dust. Some theorize that we could be a speck of dust in another universe. Our lifetime could be a few seconds in another universe. And the same goes the other direction. A speck of dust in our house could be another entire universe with a life span of a few seconds in our life.

OK, I'm already getting off track and that's too deep of a subject for what we're trying to accomplish. Maybe I'll expand on that in my next book on the theory of relativity or something really deep. Let's move on, shall we?

You can look at the world in two ways. One way is that it's very large and the other is that it's very small. We need to cover both angles to get the full picture. How's that sound?

Not so long ago the world was a lot bigger than it is today. I'm not talking about the physical size of our planet, but before there was electricity, telephones, airplanes and especially the Internet, this planet must have seemed huge. In the early stages they didn't know how big Earth was or that it was even round. Can you even imagine what those early humans were even thinking about? Talk about "you don't know what you don't know." Wow! We really can't imagine. It was probably comparable to our perception of how big the universe is today.

As time passed, we ended up here today. With all of the modern conveniences, electricity, air travel and the Internet, this planet got really small, very fast. This planet has been around for billions of years and just in the last 100 years we've made more progress in technology and modernization than the first billions of years combined? And on top of that, computer technology and the Internet have only come on board in the last forty years.

It will be mind blowing where the technology is going to be in the next few years? You better embrace it because it's not going to slow down anytime soon. Today it's hard to imagine getting into a driverless car, but it's only a matter of a few years before it'll be a common thing. It will be so natural that we'll probably be scared when we see a human driving a car going down the road. Humans make a lot more mistakes than a fine-tuned machine.

OK, let me get back to analyzing the size of our planet. Now, let's look at planet Earth as very small. If you're in outer space and you compare it to the other planets we're just a little dude. From that view it's a small world.

But wait a minute. There are approximately 7.5 billion people living on this little rock. And if you think about that way, it's easy to feel very insignificant. But don't look at it that way. The mindset you need to take is how grateful you are compared to the rest of the 7.5 billion people and how you can best help as many of those people as possible. That's 7.5 billion opportunities that are available to you.

For years I have always talked about "thinking outside the box." That's one of my big philosophies. I'm definitely an outside-of-the-box type of thinker. Sometimes I need to be kicked back into the box. Every time that you step outside of your box (or comfort zone) your box gets bigger. And bigger is better. Right?

After all of these years of talking about "thinking outside of the box," I just found another viewpoint on this. I just read Richard Branson's book, *The Virgin Way*, and he doesn't believe in thinking outside of the box, which really surprised me with his creativity, style and success. His theory is even better. He says to not let anyone build a box around you to start with. I think I like his theory better. It must be a better way to look at it since he owns his own island and I don't.

Takeaway:

Take a step back and look at the big picture. Think about what you have and don't have. Chances are that you may already have a laidback life compared to many others but you don't realize it and don't appreciate it. Use this as a starting point for the rest of the book. I know that you'll still want more and that's a good thing. You should always be learning and improving no matter what. But appreciate what you have first and go from there.

When you get stressed about something going on today ask yourself "Is it really going to make a difference tomorrow?" Sometimes the answer may be yes but just think about it before you have a heart attack over it today. It may not be worth the time and trouble today for something that may not even happen tomorrow.

Quotes:

"The big picture doesn't just come from distance; it also comes from time."
—Simon Sinek

"To change ourselves effectively, we first had to change our perceptions."
—Stephen Covey

"To the world you may be one person; but to one person you may be the world."
—Dr. Seuss

YOU CAN'T FIX EVERYTHING

Before we get too far along, I want to point out a few things to keep in mind while reading the book. YOU ARE HUMAN! YOU ARE NOT A MIRACLE WORKER! Write this down and memorize it. You can't fix everything so pick and choose your battles wisely.

It's all about being smart. If you go down the stupid trail then that's your own fault. Someone said that "you can't fix stupid" but I'm going to have to argue with them. I'm actually trying to fix it with some of the chapters in this book. OK, that's supposed to be funny but I can see where some people might read something different into that statement. Retract that. Let's not refer it as stupid. Let's refer it to it as "You don't know what you don't know." This is something that can be fixed. All you have to do is find out what you don't know.

Everyone in the world fits into the category of "You don't know what you don't know." This is one of those obvious statement but just realize that you're no exception. Face it and recognize that you're human, you don't know everything, you make mistakes, you will always make mistakes so don't beat yourself up over it. Enjoy the ride. Just be open minded, be flexible, always be learning and be coachable. Don't be rigid. Rigidity breaks. Flexible can glide you through the ups and downs and lefts and rights that you will come your way.

It's all about efficiency and being smart. Don't waste time trying to fix things that are not fixable. Sometimes things are just what they are. "It is what it is." Don't you just hate it when someone says that to you? Especially when you don't like what it is that they're talking about? Damn, that pisses me off. But we'll move on.

Don't dwell on the insignificant things and don't worry about anything that you don't have any control over. The main topics that people like to bitch about every day are politics (or the government), religion (or peoples views) and the weather. Now unless you're the Pope, the president or the big guy upstairs you don't have control over any of that. (And the Pope and president actually don't have control either but I wanted to add them in there for effect)

Now that we've established the fact that you can't fix everything, you can fix or improve yourself. You're in total control of you. There will always be circumstances that don't work out in your favor but the more important point is how you react to them. You have total control of how you react to any situation.

Takeaway:

Remember you are not perfect so get over yourself. You can't fix everything. Pick and choose your battles wisely. Work on and improve what you can and don't worry about the rest. At least not today. Tomorrow is another story.

The most important thing is to be flexible and coachable. Don't fight it Mr. Know It All. You don't know what you don't know.

Quotes:

"Don't try to solve all the world's problems. Choose your battles and fight them well. If you try to take on everything, you will succeed at nothing."
—Oliver Bancroft

"True wisdom is knowing what *you don't know.*"
—Confucius

SIMPLIFY

Yes, keep it simple. I know this isn't the first time you've heard this statement. You probably hear it all the time and you may even think about it regularly and try to live it.

But, if you get one thing out of this book I hope you get this. In my mind, this is the number one rule. Depending on your current situation, you may only need this one rule.

Always work toward simplifying everything. If it's complicated, just break it down into a bunch of simple things.

Eating an elephant

The goal is to not get overwhelmed and bog your mind down with too many things at once. Especially, insignificant things. Someone once explained to me "how to eat an elephant." The way you eat an elephant is one bite at a time. Now, eating an elephant would obviously take a long time, and if you weren't hungry it would seem even longer.

But, if you just take one bite at a time, once a day, you would eventually eat the whole elephant. Now, I'm not sure how long that would take or how it would even taste, but that doesn't matter since we're just trying to put things into perspective here.

So when you get in situations throughout the day and start getting overwhelmed and things get complicated, call a timeout. Take a few minutes and think about it. Maybe write it down and break it down into big chunks. And then take the big chunks and break those down into smaller pieces. Then work on the smaller pieces one at a time. Prioritize, work on the more important tasks first, and don't stray off the path.

Don't multitask

Now, this takes me to multitasking. A lot of people say they are good multitaskers. I think that's all bullshit. Excuse my language, but that's how strongly I feel about this. Now granted, I probably have ADD (attention deficit disorder) but I was never officially diagnosed with it fifty-plus years ago when I was younger. I think that was before they even knew what

ADD was. I probably learn to adjust and live with it as I grew older.

Just the other day I heard about a new problem: AADD. Acquired Attention Deficit Disorder. This is interesting and I can understand how it happens. We have so many distractions from the cell phone, iPad, computer, websites, etc., that it makes it hard to focus your attention even if you don't have ADD. It's crazy but it makes perfect sense. I'm sure a lot of you, like myself, get side tracked when you're online with all of the website ads and pop ups that try to get you on another website. It's not hard to have twenty webpages open at once and bounce around for hours without accomplishing what you sat down to do in the beginning.

I'm not here to talk about medical disorders. I'm bringing this up to make a point about staying focused, staying on track and recognizing how distractions can cut into simplifying your life. Recognizing the issue is half the battle and that's why I brought it up.

Let me continue talking about how I am totally against multitasking. I'm not saying it's not a challenge for me. In fact, it's one of my biggest challenges. I have to specifically concentrate on not multitasking in everything that I do. I can get sidetracked very easily on the next shiny object.

For example, I have to consciously turn my phone off, or turn the emails off to at least minimize my distractions. I'm actually writing this book, and especially this chapter, to help me as much as you. I plan to read my own book over and over and over again and refer to it more than anybody. It's my own personal guide and putting it in writing is the best way to commit things to memory and form better habits.

Speaking of distracted, I just looked down and was getting a call from my wife Janie. So I stopped writing and answered the phone. Now, that may be the right thing to do when your wife calls but it distracted me. I'm turning my phone off right now. Let me get back to my train of thought.

Here's how I like to breakdown the multitasking habit. You have four things to do. You have A, B, C and D. And if you multitask, you can get them all done in four hours. Whether you want to admit it or not, you'll be bouncing around among all four tasks. And when you're on one you'll be thinking about the others. Trust me. You will. Obviously this is dependent on what type of tasks these are, but you really can't do each task justice and give it your full focus and concentration.

Now let's continue, and imagine if you do item A and forget about B, C and D. You can be laser focused on item A and do a much better job. When you're done with task A, you move on to Task B and just rinse and repeat. You will do each one of the tasks so much better and faster than you would have if you tried to do them all at the same time.

Another advantage to this "one thing at a time concept" is that once you have truly completed a task, you can clear it from your mind and not look back. If you're really honest with yourself and you're multitasking, you're still thinking about backwards and not moving forward. If you haven't truly completed the last task, it'll still be on your little pee brain and causing stress whether you want to believe it or not. Do you see my point here? When I say "simplify," I'm talking about your mind and not just your socks and underwear still lying on the floor from last night. That is for another chapter.

This has to do with everything that you do throughout the day. Obviously some of your tasks are more important than others and you need to prioritize them. Break them down like eating that elephant again. It's really about picking and choosing your battles in order to stay focused and minimize the distractions in your mind.

I'm sure that some people are able to multitask better than others but I'm just sharing my experiences and thoughts on the subject. And it depends on what you're doing when you're multitasking. If you're talking about walking, chewing gum and talking on the cell phone that's a little bit of a different story. So you don't have to take it literally, I'm sure you can figure out when you can multitask and when it won't work for you. Just be honest with yourself. Don't think you're the busiest and most productive person on the planet just because you think you're good at it. If you are good at it, just think how much more productive you would be if you didn't do it.

Don't garbage up your mind. Do me a favor, throughout the day, as you are bouncing off the walls trying to do more than one (thinking) task at a time, just stop. Take a timeout and breathe and then think about what I've said in this chapter.

Fighting an army:

Another example or metaphor of multitasking is if you were trying to fight an army by yourself.

Obviously if you had to go up against all of them at once, you would get your ass kicked very quickly. But if you had the opportunity to fight each of them, one at a time, at least you'd have some kind of chance. And if you were in tip-top shape with a lot of endurance, you might have a chance to beat each of them and subsequently beat an army all by yourself.

Now, this is an extreme and probably unrealistic example but you do run into armies every day. Granted, you may create some of these armies yourself, so just don't do that. You'll run into enough armies in your day-to-day life without creating them. Don't forget that you can't fix everything.

Takeaway:

Keep your life simple by starting with your thoughts and actions. Don't over complicate things. It's your life. Live it your way but simplify it your way.

Keep your mind clear and focused by breaking down the big jobs into little tasks. Prioritize those tasks and take care of them one at a time until the goal is accomplished. Try not to mulitask or allow distraction to become a habit.

Life can be very simple if you want it to b
you have to be aware and identify the complica
in your life that you have control over. Notice, that
said, "what you have control over." Don't even think
about it if you can't change it. You'll just attract
more complication to your life if you go after the
impossible.

Once you identify the complicated areas that you
can change, getting past them will be much easier.
It's not as hard as you might think if you are aware
of what your challenges actually are. Just maintain
the right attitude and mindset and don't make it
more complicated than it is. Work on simplifying all
areas of your life. You can do it.

Quotes:

"Life is really simple, but we insist on making it
complicated."
—Confucius

"Simplicity is the ultimate sophistication."
—Leonardo da Vinci

"Gentlemen, I do one thing at a time. I do it very
well. And then I move on."
—Major Charles Emerson Winchester III, *M*A*S*H*

GET ORGANIZED

I realize that everyone is different and getting organized is easier for some people than others. You don't have to be totally anal about it if that doesn't come natural to you. But there are a few little tricks that can help anyone. Just having some thoughts in the back of your mind after reading this chapter will move you in the right direction. Or at least in a direction that will make things a little easier.

Now, being organized is kind of my thing. In fact, I've been called "Anal Al" by more than a few people. My mom was very organized and kept everything very neat. I don't know if I've always been organized when I was younger but it's definitely grown on me now.

My wife Janie says that she thought she was organized until she met me. She actually was organized before we met but not on the extreme level as me. So now we're both getting older and getting more anal as the years go by. We ought to be a real joy to hang out with as we get into our senior years.

Being organized helps productivity by reducing clutter in your mind. It's easy to get a cluttered mind very quickly if you're not on top of it. If you're not a naturally organized person (which most people aren't) at least I can give you a few pointers to help you along the way.

Being organized and simplifying are the two main traits to having a laidback lifestyle.

Car keys:

I don't like to clutter up my mind trying to remember things. I have enough things on my mind without adding a bunch of little things. For example, if I want to remember something to take when I'm leaving the office or home, I always put it with my car keys. I can't leave the house or the office without my keys. Duh!

I always have a specific place to put my car keys at the house and also at the office. I put them in the same place every time. And I mean every time. There's nothing worse than some crazy person running around always looking for their car keys.

Just a little pet peeve of mine. That's where I put my wallet as well. So if there's anything that comes across my mind throughout the day or evening that I don't want to forget when I leave, I put it right beside my keys and my wallet.

Thin billfold with one card:

Speaking of my wallet or as I call showing my old age, my billfold. Which my wife really thinks funny and it's something our grandparents would probably say. I used to carry a lot of things in my billfold, like photos and a lot of credit cards.

But now my wallet (yes it's a wallet now) is very, very thin. I might have a twenty in it just in case but most of the time I don't even carry cash. There's no point in it unless I'm going to the airport or somewhere I need to tip for the service. Apart from a couple of dollars, the only other things I have in my wallet is my insurance card, my driver's license and one credit card. That's it, and I keep it in my front pocket. Years ago, my chiropractor told me that carrying a big fat wallet around in my back pocket was the worst thing anyone can do to get your hips out of alignment. So I went "thin" on the wallet and carry it in my front pocket.

Use technology:

What has helped organization and minimizing the wallet situation is our smartphones. You gotta love technology. And I do love technology. Some people are just old-fashioned and hate technology. They say they can't keep up with it. It is hard to keep up with it as fast as it's moving but my suggestion is you better keep up with it as much as possible. You better not only keep up with it but you need to embrace it. It will make life easier.

There are so many apps out there for your phone and computer to make life easier and get organized. I can go on and on about apps to organize your files and your life as a whole. But then on the other hand, you have to minimize those apps and websites or you'll just be all over the place. It's so easy to start website searching and then you get these pop-ups and you flash over to that one, then you get another pop up and you flash over to that one. I know I mentioned this before in a previous chapter but it is something that I have to fight all of the time so I'm not only repeating this for you but for me. To be honest, I'm actually getting more out of writing this book than I would have ever imagined. By putting it on paper it really makes me stop and think about this stuff even more than I did before. OK, now I got off on another tangent. Let's get back to my point.

If you're not into all of the applications and technology that's OK. Just find one that you can use for your notes, calendar, reminders, etc., for organizing your life. Then pick one and stick to it. Don't try to use more than one. That's back to that multitasking thing and don't do it.

I use Google for about everything to stay organized. My email, calendar, tasks, photos and documents. In fact, I'm actually dictating my book and letting Google transcribe my first draft, so I can get my thoughts out and pull it all together later. It's easy to keep track of everything on one platform, plus I can share what I want with others to collaborate. I'm not sure how secure any of the online (cloud) stuff is but it keeps them all together in one place. If the National Security Administration wants to know more about me I'm sure they can find out whether I'm on the cloud or not. I'm not recommending you use Google apps or not it just works best for me right now. Play around, find what you like, and use something to keep yourself more organized.

Get rid of junk.

I am a big proponent of getting rid of junk. My definition of junk is things that you don't need. I used to hang on to stuff forever in case I might need it someday. Most of the time "someday" never came. I paid for a storage unit for ten years and hardly ever visited my supposedly important stuff. I'm not down playing with family heir looms and memory boxes but most of the stuff I stored for years was not that important. A cluttered house or office is a cluttered mind. Less is more in many cases.

Sock Drawers

I do have to admit that Anal Al is a little extreme when it comes to having a neat and tidy house and work area. Sock and underwear drawers are neatly stacked, hanging cloths are in order and spaced out accordingly, files are organized and so on. You get the picture.

When I first moved into my condo (before Janie moved in), she thought it was fun to show our friends around my place to see my sock drawers and closets. A few of them thought it would be fun to rearrange my sock drawers. It was all fun and games until my drawers were unorganized. We still laugh about that.

Janie and her daughter, Sara, would call my condo "The Hospital" because it was so neat and sterile. Looking back at pictures they were exactly right. I'm a guy. There were no plants, greenery or any color in the place for that matter. The carpet was a light cream color, the furniture was black and everything was in line like an army barracks. We still laugh about that today.

Yes, I admit that I may be a little compulsive on the organizational stuff but I'm getting more flexible as life goes on thanks to Janie. And Janie has plants and colorful things all around the place now. It does look much better and not so clinical.

Takeaway:

I'm not saying go out there and change your habits overnight. Be realistic. I don't expect you to: have a real thin wallet, use your car keys as a guide, have your sock drawer exactly organized in color and have your hanging clothes exactly two inches apart all color coordinated in one day. That's crazy talk. Even though I do that, I still think it is a little odd.

Practice one little piece at a time. Whatever you don't want to forget to take to the office tomorrow put it beside your car keys.

If being organized does not come natural for you, don't worry about it. Anyone can learn to be organized with a little practice. Being organized will unclutter your brain and increase your productivity. If you can unclutter your brain, your life will follow. I'm going to share more ways to unclutter your brain in the next few chapters.

So go start getting your shit together.

Oh, and by the way. Don't leave home without making the bed. If your day doesn't start off organized you'll always be trying to catch up.

Quotes:

"Clutter is the physical manifestation of unmade decisions fueled by procrastination"
—Christina Scalise, *Organize Your Life and More*

"For every minute spent in organizing, an hour is earned."
—Benjamin Franklin

FIND YOUR PASSION!

Life is too short to do what you hate. This chapter is about finding and doing what you are passionate about, or at the very least, making you realize what you need to do to be happy. Your life really should be fun.

How good you are at something is usually directly related to how much you love or hate it. If you love what you're doing, then doing it well just comes naturally. A difficult problem doesn't feel as hard when you really enjoy trying to solve it. On the other hand if you force yourself to do what you don't like or even hate, you'll either be bad at it, or it'll take every bit of your energy to do it in an average way. People do this every day because they think they're supposed to be doing it for one reason or another. Does that make sense?

This is one of the most important chapters you need to think about. Everyone wants to live a happy life, but most people end up doing what they think they're supposed to do according to others and never follow their passion.

How do you find your passion? That's a very good question and it's obviously a different answer for everyone. Only you can answer that question. Many people know what their passion is but can't always find a way to do it and make a living.

Times are changing my friends. No matter what your passion, there are infinite ways to make a living doing what you love due to the internet. I'll expand on this later.

Whether you're an entrepreneur or an employee, it doesn't matter. Figure out what you like to do and go do it.

Don't try to put a round peg in a square hole. Think about that when you are managing people or outsourcing to others as well. Figure out what people are good at and then assign tasks or place them in those positions. You'll get the most productivity out of your team and they will enjoy it more as well.

Many managers try to force their employees into doing a job that they're not good at and then are surprised they don't do a very good job. That is very frustrating for everyone. If there are times when you absolutely have to delegate a job to someone who is not a natural at the task, then manage your expectations and work with them together to figure it out.

Do what you do best and let others do what they do best. Once you figure this out life will be much easier for everyone.

Use your time wisely. Your time has value. Figure out what that value is and if you can outsource something more efficiently (especially if you hate doing it) then do it. As an example, "I don't work on cars". Enough said about that.

Your life is like a jigsaw puzzle. If you take all of the pieces of the puzzle and dump them on the table it's just a pile of little cardboard pieces that make no sense. But when you take the time to find each piece and put it in the right place, it will create a wonderful picture.

Another way to look at this is if you're doing what you love, then you're using the best tools in your own personal toolbox. When you're doing that, you're being the best you can be and are not cheating yourself or others around you of what you have to offer.

Sit back and think about what you're good at and passionate about, and go change some things. Obviously, you can't change things over night. Everything is a work in progress. But start taking the steps forward and think about your way to the next step.

You're not only cheating yourself, but you're cheating everyone around you if you're not truly living your passion and contributing to the world with the best cards you've been dealt. I'm not saying this to be mean. I'm saying this to light a fire under your ass to really give this some serious thought.

You're either an asset or a liability so you might as well be an asset and be the best asset you can be.

If it's worth doing it's worth overdoing.

"If it's worth doing it's worth overdoing" is another one of my Al-isms, which my friends hear me say all of the time. If you're doing what you love, overdoing it becomes a lot easier.

I do feel the need to clarify myself here. The literal term of "over doing" something is not always a good thing. What I'm really saying with my Al-ism statement is to find your passion and go after it with every fiber of your being. Do it with laser focus and a "never give up" attitude.

Don't cheat yourself by just dipping your toes in the water. Dive right in and be all in.

I do it in my engineering career at SEI, I did it when I got back into the real estate investing business 8 years ago and I'm doing it now writing this book.

Here's a tip on staying motivated when you set a goal. Share your goal with others. It's about accountability. As soon as I shared my plans of writing this book with my friends, family and on Facebook, I had no choice in my mind but to finish and publish it. That, my friends, is jumping out of your comfort zone from 5,000 feet up without a parachute. Try it sometime.

One more tip about finding your passion and going after your dreams. Don't forget to BE YOURSELF. This might sound simple but it's very easy to want to be like someone else and then try to act like them or be them. Yes, find mentors, coaches and people that you admire whose accomplishments you want to match or exceed, but don't try to be them. Be yourself and do it your way. Just like one of my favorite Fleetwood Mac songs, "Go Your Own Way."

Takeaway:

Go out there, be yourself and find your passion. And then when you figure it out, dig deep and do it with every ounce of positive energy that you have.

Once you get through the rest of the chapter in this book, come back to this chapter and think about what you can offer the world. You'll be amazed at what you come up with.

Remember, "If it's worth doing, it's worth overdoing." So go out there and over do it. Follow your heart, go after your dreams, never give up, persevere and most of all enjoy the ride.

Quotes:

"Working hard for something we don't care about is called stress; working hard for something we love is called passion."
—Simon Sinek

"Your work is going to fill a large part of your life, and the only way to be truly satisfied is to do what you believe is great work. And the only way to do great work is to love what you do."
—Steve Jobs

"Never continue in a job you don't enjoy. If you're happy in what you're doing, you'll like yourself, you'll have inner peace. And if you have that, along with physical health, you will have had more success than you could possibly have imagined."
—Johnny Carson

"The art of delegation is one of the key skills any entrepreneur must master."
—Richard Branson

"People should pursue what they're passionate about. That will make them happier than pretty much anything else."
—Elon Musk

BE POSITIVE

This chapter is not only to tell you to be positive, but to show you how to become positive and stay positive. I realize that this is not the first time you've heard someone tell you to be positive. In fact, most of the ideas in this book are things that you've heard before. None of it is rocket science. It's all common sense.

I'm just putting it all together in a simple, easy-to-read book. The easier I make this book to read, the more likely that you'll retain the information and act on it. Some of it is so simple that it's more of a wake-up call to things you already knew, but just haven't gotten around practicing them yet.

I know it's not easy to always be positive and it's even harder to stay positive sometimes. You can't tell yourself to be positive and *poof!,* you're positive. It's like the rest of the tips in this book. They're all something we have to study, be aware of, work on and learn. These are all just seeds to plant in your mind.

We all know people that have a hard time being positive at all. Some people just can't do it. I'm naturally a positive person and have been my whole life. So if you got advice from someone that is naturally positive, I'm sure that you would say, "That's easy for you to do." And you might be right but I think if someone really goes after it, reads the right books or listens to the right people, anyone can have a positive attitude. If you really want to have and keep a positive attitude, then go figure out a way that works for you. You can start by appreciating all of the good things that you have and expand on it from there.

Avoid negativity

The first thing I would suggest is to avoid negativity like the plague. I know you can't get rid of all of it. That's impossible. But get rid of or avoid as much negativity as humanly possible. You may not think you can, but it's much easier to accomplish than you think. I'm talking about avoiding negative people, avoiding the negative news, and so on and so forth. Now, you can't just say "Beam me up, Scotty" and avoid this, but you can pick and choose your battles.

Avoiding it all together is impossible but at least recognize it when it is in your face and most importantly control how you react to it.

If I'm around negativity, I try to let it go in one ear and out the other. That is definitely something that takes practice. Let the negativity pass through your little head, passing quickly through your brain matter and try not to let any of it stick to your attitude on the way through. You don't have to get emotionally involved.

Totally avoiding the negative news is not realistic, but what you can do is to take a different viewpoint on it. All of the TV news shows and newspapers are about the ratings. That's just their business and it's about the bottom line, like any other business. They dramatize it to get ratings. I'm not saying to ignore the bad news, just take it in with a grain of salt if you can. Don't dwell on it. I'm not saying not to worry or be concerned about anything either. By all means, if you can help out a certain situation, it is your obligation to help out any situation or anybody that you can. On the same token, if you don't have control over it, don't let it control your life.

I also avoid conversations about religion and politics. First of all, I'm not that knowledgeable on either subject. And they usually turn into a debate. I'm not really into debating, but I know that lawyers actually go to school for that stuff and some people enjoy it. Not me. I'm usually not the smartest person in the room, and if I were, I would not throw it out there for all to see. There's usually at least one person in the room that thinks he's the smartest, so I let him go with it. It usually turns out they are not as smart as they think they are.

Don't talk about other people negatively

Another thing to evaluate about yourself is how you talk about other people when you're not around them. We all have friends who are always talking about other people negatively. I always wonder, if they are talking to someone that way to me, are they talking negatively about me when I'm not around? They probably are.

That's the nature of some people. If you catch yourself talking negatively about someone else, just think about that. Nothing good comes from that. People who do that are typically insecure and are trying to make themselves feel better or look better to others. It works just the opposite.

Look at yourself in the mirror and think about what you're saying to someone: are you the person always complaining and always whining about something? Are you projecting a negative or a positive feeling toward people when you're talking to them? Keep that in mind so when you have a conversation you are projecting a positive attitude, and people will want to keep talking to you.

Also look at someone when they're talking to you, and ask yourself, "Is this person having a positive or negative affect on me right now?" I know that's weird to say but think about that the next time you are around someone. You might think differently about them now. If they're negative, then try to take them to a better place and change the tone of the conversation. If that doesn't work, just run!

Some people are genuinely about helping others and some are all about themselves. I call the people that are all about themselves the "ME ME ME" people. They are pretty easy to identify once you know what you're looking for.

One more comment about being negative. **Don't be a drama queen.** Nobody wants to hear all about someone's over-zealous reaction, embellishment and usually misguided opinion of something someone else did or said. Stay calm. Don't be one of those over dramatized news reporters on TV. Just give me the facts, man.

Attract positivity

You are going to attract more friends by being a positive person. People want to be around positive people, it's just the way it is. You are what you attract. If you're positive, you're going to attract more positive people. If you're positive and you are with a negative person, it should up lift them to some degree, unless their negativity is much stronger than your positivity. Then that sucks. If you have to change the subject because they're talking negatively, then do it. If you continue talking positive, it might make them think about how negative they are. Over power them with positivity and kindness if you have to. Stay strong my friend.

You can't fix everybody. Pick and choose your battles. Know when to move on and quit wasting your time on a lost cause. Don't let negative people drag you down.

Positive people attract positive people. Positivity is a lot more fun and less stressful. I'm no doctor but I think having a positive attitude would help you live longer. Even if I'm wrong on that fact, being positive is a lot more fun and it's a hell of a lot more fun for your friends while you're still around as well. Don't be a Debbie Downer.

Takeaway:

Face it, some people are like clouds. When they disappear it's a beautiful day.

Negativity and positivity are both contagious and can be spread very easily and fast. So be mindful about what you spread.

Be positive. I know it's not easy to stay frigging positive every single day but if you are aware of the positive attitude you want to have it will make it easier to obtain. It will make the people's lives around you much better as well. They won't be sitting around talking about how negative you are.

Remember, when you start to get down on someone for not being who you think they should be, or get sucked into the negative conversations, step back and call a time out. **Don't let yourself get sucked into a negative person's world.**

Be someone that people enjoy being around. Take a look at yourself and evaluate if you are a positive, upbeat person that never talks about anyone, or if you are a Debbie Downer. Take stock and think about it.

The Debbie Downers that I know don't think they're Debbie Downers at all. My point is that it is not always obvious from within. You have to be brutally honest with yourself. It is easy to get into the habit of negativity and jumping on the band wagon of talking about other people in a negative way. It is human nature to go along with the crowd but it's not the right thing to do. Be your own positive person no matter what the crowd is saying.

Quotes:

"Once you replace negative thoughts with positive ones, you'll start having positive results."
—Willie Nelson

"Positive anything is better than negative nothing."
—Elbert Hubbard

"In every day, there are 1,440 minutes. That means we have 1,440 daily opportunities to make a positive impact."
—Les Brown

"Send out a cheerful, positive greeting, and most of the time you will get back a cheerful, positive greeting. It's also true that if you send out a negative greeting, you will, in most cases, get back a negative greeting."

–Zig Ziglar

Virtually nothing is impossible in this world if you just put your mind to it and maintain a positive attitude."

–Lou Holtz

EMBRACE PROGRESS

A few months ago I was visiting one of my older friends. She's about 85 years old. She was giving me her opinion on how bad it is in today's world and that her mother would not have believed all of the things going on today. She was referring to all of the bad news like terrorism, drugs, violence, sex offenders, etc. She thought it was better back when she was growing up. I'm sure that she remembered it as simpler times and I didn't argue with her.

But the fact is, today is the best time to be alive in history. Yeah, I know you hear about all of the bad things going on but most of them were all going on before. We didn't have access to that kind of information back in the day.

On the same hand, we didn't have access to the good information that we have now either. There's more ways to make money than ever before and to learn as much as you want on the internet. And most of it is free. It's a matter of concentrating on the good instead of the bad. There's more information available than ever before. We all have a choice on how to accept it and use it.

Do you want to concentrate on the negative stuff or the positive stuff? If you're reading this book you already know that this is a stupid question. Who would pick the negative answer? Well, some people do just naturally without realizing it.

Someone who is negative (a fixed-mindset person) is going to view the world as a terrible place based on all of the bad things going on.

While the positive (the growth-mindset person), is going to get online every day and suck up the good, positive, self-improvement stuff like a sponge. The fixed-mindset versus growth-mindset is from the book *Mindsets: The New Psychology of Success* by Carol S. Dweck. Check it out. It's worth the read (or listen to it on Audible like I do).

Another point that I made about being alive today in 2017 is that a man's average age is 86 and a woman's is 92. One hundred years ago, in 1917, the average age for a man was 48 and a woman was 54. I love being alive today.

Social media:

As you can tell by now, I'm all about technology to make life simpler and more efficient. I'm a geek at heart. I'm also embracing the social media stuff and how it can help your business. It is not just about posting party pictures on Facebook, even though I do that now and then. I'm talking about really reaching an audience for your service or product all over the world. It's amazing.

Social media is a very powerful marketing tool. I'm not going to elaborate on this for now. I'll save that for a future book but if our president is doing it then it must be the right thing. OK, this is my sick sense of humor coming out again.

Seriously, if you're not into social media for business at least check it out, keep an open mind and investigate it further. Embrace it.

Take away:

Embrace progress and the lives that we have today because of it. The next time someone complains to you about new technology, or the construction and congestion that is going on due to progress, remind them that it's a heck of a lot better to be alive now than 150 years ago. Don't take what we have today for granted. Thank your ancestors for paving the way.

Today, we can sit in a seat on a plane with a cocktail and a meal and go from one side of the world to the other. I love this place (and time). It'll even get better in the future but we're not there yet, so we'll cross that bridge when we get to it.

Quotes:

"Progress is impossible without change, and those who cannot change their minds cannot change anything."
—George Bernard Shaw

"Growth is the great separator between those who succeed and those who do not. When I see a person beginning to separate themselves from the pack, it's almost always due to personal growth."
—John C. Maxwell

LIVE WITHIN YOUR MEANS

This is one of my simple common-sense chapters like all of the rest, but if you want to live a stressful life, spend more money than you make. I know this is not telling you anything you don't already know, but it's just one of those important points that I had to put it in this book. If you don't correct this situation I can guarantee that you will never accomplish that laidback life that we're talking about.

I know a lot of people in the world live beyond their means thanks to credit cards and loans. And at the risk of stating the obvious, which is what most of my book does, I'm going to say it anyway. There are only two solutions to solving this problem.

Lower your expenses or increase your income. It's not rocket science my friends.

Lower your expenses

When I was growing up, my mom and grandparents always said, "Don't try to keep up with the Joneses." Now, I don't know who these Jones people were because I never met them, but we'll call them our neighbors for the sake of this story. The point of the story was not to spend more money than you can afford to impress other people. It is crazy when you think about it. You're trying to keep up with someone else to impress them, when in reality you probably didn't know much about them anyway. Your neighbors might have been spending more than they could afford to impress you. They might have been so far under water and upside down on their bills that they were stressed out. And thinking back about our neighbors when I was growing up, they were as far from laidback as anyone that I knew.

Cutting your expenses, especially if you've been accustomed to a certain lifestyle for a long time, is not easily done without compromising your lifestyle. But it is possible if you figure out what you really need to make you happy, and what expenses you have because of that infamous Jones family next door.

Everyone can cut some kind of expenses if they need to. It might take some creative, outside-of-the-box thinking, but you can do it. And if you're not very good with finances there's a lot of free help and assistance out there in the world or online. Go look for it, accept it, and don't stick your head in the sand. This stuff does not fix itself.

Increase your income

The other solution to this situation is to increase your income. There is a future chapter in this book that addresses increasing your earning potential, so I won't spoil the details on that one yet. But besides making yourself more valuable, there's a lot of ways today to make additional money online in your spare time. I'm not going into a lot of details here but I could, and that would be an entire book. Just Google stuff. You'll be surprised what's out there and how often you can do it from the comfort of your own home.

One great way to make additional income and contribute to others at the same time is to be a **coach or mentor**. No matter what you've done in your life and no matter how old you are, everyone has experiences that someone else can benefit from.

Age difference does not matter. A 70-year-old person can benefit from the experiences of a 20-year-old and vice versa. By being a coach or mentor, you will not only be helping others but you will also learn from your students.

There are always ways you can increase your income. Figure out what value you can bring to someone else.

I hope this helps. Again, this is not rocket science but it's another one of those little nuggets that can improve your life, attitude and mindset. It sure would ease the stress if you can eliminate the **too much month left at the end of the money** situation.

Takeaway:

Think about ways to cut your expenses, but better yet, think about ways to increase your income. There's no better way to live a laidback life than to make more money than you spend.

Think how relaxed you'll be if you can wake up every morning and say to yourself, "I've got money I haven't spent yet." That doesn't mean that you have to run right out and spend it either.

If your finances are causing you stress, then make it your goal to fix them. Don't sit around and wish for more money. That won't work, and neither will playing the lottery. Get online and start searching your options based on your experience and talents. And most of all keep in mind what you're passionate about. Make this fun.

Quotes

"Money isn't everything unless you don't have any, then it seems to become everything."
—T. Harv Eker

"It's not that things cost too much it's just that you don't make enough money."
—Jim Rohn

"Get going. Move forward. Aim high. Plan a takeoff. Don't just sit on the runway and hope someone will come along and push the airplane. It simply won't happen. Change your attitude and gain some altitude. Believe me, you'll love it up here."
—Donald J. Trump

TREAT OTHERS LIKE YOU WANT TO BE TREATED

This is my number one, and I mean my number one rule. I know I have several number one rules but this is really number one. Seriously. HA!

Always treat others like you would like to be treated. I'm talking about family, close friends, distant friends, acquaintances, and total strangers that you come across, every moment of every day.

Don't do it expecting something in return. Do it unconditionally. If you do it expecting something in return, you're probably going to be disappointed. People are going to disappoint you, especially if you keep your expectations high.

Don't brag about being nice or treating people nicer than you think that they deserve either. In fact, don't brag about anything. Actions speak the loudest. If you have to brag about something that you've done to remind people, then you didn't do a very good job of what you're bragging about anyway.

Don't make the mistake of expecting immediate gratification for your actions either. It will always come back to you eventually, even if it's only in your mind.

Don't be judgmental

My mom was the most non-judgmental person there was and she treated everyone the same. It's not always easy but it's something to consider when you're starting to get an attitude towards someone.

I wish everybody was like my mom but they aren't, and I don't lose sleep over it. Some people can't help judging others. Everybody knows someone that just has to judge others or think their way is the right way. We are really seeing it even more on the news now with the new presidential situation but I'm not going there.

You can't honestly judge other people fairly if you haven't experienced life exactly like they have.

Don't talk bad about people.

We talked about this in a previous chapter, and how talking about other people just spreads negativity. We all know them. Some people can't help it. And I know that we've all been guilty of this. I know some of it is just human nature.

But stop it. Or at least think about it the next time you find yourself doing it. It does nobody any good. When someone is talking bad about someone else it's usually about them trying to make themselves look better than the person that they're talking about.

As I listen to the people that are constantly talking bad about someone else you can't help but wonder what they're saying about me when I'm not around. If they're talking about all of these other people all of the time, then I'm pretty sure that I'm not the only perfect person that they know. You get what I'm saying here.

When you talk bad about other people it makes you look bad and reduces your credibility. The stories may not even be true or at least you don't know all of the circumstances that lead up to these actions. It's no fun to hear that someone has been talking about you, so don't talk about other people, don't spread the negativity and don't judge.

Road rage story

Until you've walked in somebody else's shoes, you don't know where they've been. I'm always reminded of the story about a road rage incident where a person is driving down the street and this truck comes up behind them, swirls around them honking and zigzagging. Everyone in the cars around are very upset, and rightfully so. They're all yelling from their cars about how this guy is crazy and he's a lunatic and he's inconsiderate of others.

Well it turned out that the guy in the truck driving crazy had just received a call that his son was in a terrible accident and was in the hospital in critical condition. He was obviously, as any of us would be, in panic mode. I'm not saying he should have been driving like that and putting other people in danger, but his mindset at that time was off the charts.

That might be a little drastic of an example but I'm just making a point. Stop and think about it the next time you get upset about someone else's actions. They just might be having a worst day than you are.

Assholes are everywhere.

I'm not saying there are not assholes out there in the world because they are very abundant. I thought they were only at the places I hang out, but I've come to find out over many years that they're everywhere. Sometimes you can't get away from them. It's like *The Walking Dead* at times. Assholes are everywhere but I'm not judging.

Even if the person has not had a bad day and is naturally an asshole, don't let that affect you either. That's their problem. Don't let their problem affect your day and more importantly your life. Smile and wish them a nice day. You should always treat them the way you'd like to be treated, even if you know they won't treat you nicely in return.

If you don't agree with someone's actions or they pissed you off in some way, don't try to punish them. Take the high road and look at ways that you might be able to help them get on a better track or help their attitude and mindset. How people treat others is a direct reflection of how they feel about themselves.

Give compliments

Don't be stingy with compliments. Give sincere and genuine compliments freely when they are due. When you compliment someone it can go a long way. You can always make someone's day a little better. And more likely than not, they will pass that attitude on to someone else and it will grow from there. You never know how the impact of your behavior toward one person will affect many more lives. This can work in a positive or negative way so just make sure that you're spreading positivity.

Giving compliments will not only help others but will help you as well. It feels good to give compliments and make someone's day.

But also accept compliments:

It's as important to accept compliments, as it is to give them. Don't try to be modest when someone gives you a compliment, and say it was no big deal or something like that. Just say "Thank you" and accept the compliment. After all, you don't want to deprive someone else from feeling good about giving out compliments either.

Takeaway

This goes beyond just treating others like you want to be treated. It's an attitude in the way that you think of and speak to others. You do not know what goes on in the mind of another or what motivates another's actions. You can't change others so just work on yourself.

Treat others like you want to be treated. Don't be judgmental, even if they are an asshole. And don't talk about people negatively behind their back. If you do then you'll be the asshole in someone else's eyes that just read this book. Got it!

Quotes:

"How people treat you is their karma; how you react is yours."
—Wayne Dyer

"Life is too short for long-term grudges."
—Elon Musk

"Be kind, for everyone you meet is fighting a hard battle."
—Philo

"Take time to be kind and to say 'thank you.'"
—Zig Ziglar

"People don't care how much you know until they know how much you care."
—Theodore Roosevelt

LIVE AND LET LIVE

L ive your own life and don't worry about how other people are living. Whether it's race, religion, politics or sexual preference, it does not matter. If they are not hurting another human being, then "Live and Let Live." End of sentence. It's that simple to me. It's not up for debate. Get frigging over it.

If you don't like how somebody lives or how they act, that's fine. I'm not suggesting that you hang out with them and be BFF's or anything. You're going to hang out with people that you have things in common anyway. Don't worry about the rest of the world.

Arms length

You can't be expected to like everyone or have something in common with everyone. In fact, we can really only count our closest friends on one hand, as they say. So if our closest friends are only a handful of people, then that means there are 7.5 billion people in the world minus your five friends that are not your closest friends. What they heck do we do about those other 7.5 billion people?

Well, I'll tell you. If you want, you can keep them all at arms length. Now, I'm just kidding about the 7 billion people in the world. You obviously don't know the rest of the world and will likely come in contract with only a small percentage of them. But I am referring to to the majority of the people that are not your best-friends-forever types.

My suggestion is to keep them at arm's length. If they don't fit into your mold, then don't hang out with them and bitch about it. There's nothing wrong with not having everyone as your best friend. You probably don't match their mold either. That's just life. But the point is that you care about all of them.

Don't judge them and don't gossip about them if they don't act exactly like you think they should act. If everyone were a clone it would be a very boring and terrible world. Don't stress out and judge others because someone else is not like you or doesn't have the same opinions as you do.

I have a lot of friends and I'm very proud of that. People say to me quite often "Big Al, how do you know so many people and have so many friends?". And my standard response is: "It's because I'm not very picky with who I hang out with."

Now, that's a joke, but there's some truth to that. I like to think that I'm able to get along very well with about anyone no matter what.

Takeaway:

Take a chill pill. Don't judge others and get your panties in a bunch because someone is not living the way you think they should live. That's just bullshit. Live your life on how you want to live and let others live theirs. Both sides will be much happier that way.

And just a heads-up! The quote below is probably my favorite one of the book so read it.

Quotes:

"So I say, 'Live and let live.' That's my motto. 'Live and let live.' And anyone who can't go along with that, take him outside and shoot the motherfucker. It's a simple philosophy, but it's always worked in our family."

—George Carlin

You've got to have a sense of humor!

BE A PART OF THE SOLUTION

Another one of my Al-isms is "If you're not part of the solution then you're part of the problem." I've said that for a long time but never really knew who said it until I started writing this book. So before I went too far with this chapter, I thought I'd find out and give him credit. The guy that said this is Eldridge Cleaver. He was a writer and activist. You can Google him if you want to know more but, I just wanted to give him credit for this since I didn't come up with the saying myself.

It's pretty simple to figure out. It's either black or white. Always try to be contributing in a positive way in all parts of your life. It goes hand-in-hand with being a positive person as opposed to a negative one.

Now, I do have a knack for solving problems. Maybe it has to do with my engineering background or me being anal. It's probably a little of both. Either way, I'm very good at seeing the big picture, analyzing it, breaking it down into little pieces in a calm manner and usually with a sense of humor, and then attacking the problems. Look at every problem as an opportunity. We share a similar viewpoint when we are betting on our golf match. "Every shot makes someone happy."

This concept of problem solving doesn't come naturally to a lot of people so it is something, like many of the other chapters that you can work toward. It's a behavior or habit that if you're aware of it, you can study, practice and learn how to react to any situation in a positive way. And possibly make a contribution to the solution. I want to bring a little awareness to your thought process when you run into a challenging situation.

I'm sure you all know or work with people that are down right negative. I'm a pretty patient person most of the time, but sometimes it's hard. I'm working on that. My pet peeve is when someone comes up to me and says, "We can't do this" or "This can't be done." My initial response is to start kicking the shit out of them. But in reality, I've never been in a fight in my life so I'm just saying that to give you a level of my frustration with that response.

But I do respond in a sarcastic way by saying "OK, we'll just call the client and tell him we can't do the project and they should go to our competition to solve it for them." That does bring some awareness to their comment and gets them to think about it differently.

Granted, maybe what the client has requested is impossible, but let's take a look from all angles of the client's end goal. If it is truly impossible then our clients or competition won't be able to do it either so we might as well take the high road and explore what we can do to help the client.

The first thing to do is to find alternate solutions and possibilities, and have some options for the client to consider when informing them of the situation. Don't just go in and tell them "It can't be done." That's no answer. Don't tell them what you can't do, tell them what you can do. It's all in the presentation. Put a positive perspective on a negative situation.

After all, our client came to us to solve their problem. In fact, all businesses are about solving problems. For example, in our engineering business, the client may need a new silo or conveyor built. He doesn't want to build it for his health. He's obviously got a problem to solve. Now, it may not be a bad problem, he may have to expand his production or storage capacity because their business is doing better than expected. This is where you replace the word "problem" with "opportunity." In this case the client has an opportunity but his problem is that he doesn't know how to solve it. Or he doesn't have the resources to solve it. Let me put it another way.

Selling hamburgers

If you're selling hamburgers, the problem that you're going to be solving for your customers when they come in the door is they're hungry. So you can solve their problem by selling them a hamburger. This is about a simple as it gets.

So somebody comes in to your hamburger stand and they're hungry but they want a hot dog. Well you don't make hot dogs. You could just say "That's too bad for you, we don't have hot dogs here." That's a little over dramatic statement, but you get where I'm going with this. The correct and positive way to handle this is to tell them that you only serve hamburgers but there's a great hot dog stand about a mile down the street.

Now it's up to them. They'll definitely appreciate it that you unselfishly gave them options to solving their problem, and either walk a mile to get their hot dog and or they'll say screw it and order one of your tasty hamburgers because you were so nice about it. Either way, you helped them solve their problem.

Our real estate deals have 5 winners

It's the same with any business. Every deal has to be a win-win situation or it won't work. I started my real estate investing business eight years ago.

My business model is simple. We find motivated sellers that will take an all-cash offer for a quick-closing in as-is condition. We use private lenders to fund the projects. We hire contractors to fix the house up. We sell it on a rent-to-own basis to buyers that may not be able to get financing right away, and the neighbors are happy that the ugly house on their block is not ugly anymore.

All 5 parties are winners:

#1. The Sellers got rid of his problem property quickly with no hassle.

#2 The Private Lender gets a great return on his money secured by a mortgage.

#3 The Contractors made a profit, created jobs and purchased goods and materials.

#4 The Tenant/Buyers got a nice house that may not have otherwise been available to them.

#5 The Neighborhood got rid of the ugly house on the street and increased their home value.

It is a very good feeling when you can create something like this to help everyone.

Takeaway:

No matter what situation you find yourself in, you always have choices. When you come to a fork in the road you can go the positive way and be part of the solution or take the negative route and add to the problem.

Keep an open mind, be creative, and be the damn problem solver. If you are passionate about something and it can solve a problem, you may have a life-changing business opportunity in front of you. Think about that statement.

Quotes:

"When you show deep empathy toward others, their defensive energy goes down, and positive energy replaces it. That's when you can get more creative in solving problems."
—Stephen Covey

"The mind is like a parachute. It doesn't work if it isn't open."
—Frank Zappa

"Whatever the problem, be part of the solution. Don't just sit around raising questions and pointing out obstacles. We've all worked with that person. That person is a drag."
—Tina Fey

"What is the difference between an obstacle and an opportunity? Our attitude toward it. Every opportunity has a difficulty, and every difficulty has an opportunity."
—J. Sidlow Baxter

You can have everything in life you want, if you'll just help enough other people get what they want."
—Zig Ziglar

CONTRIBUTE

Throughout every day of your life, you should always strive to be contributing something. Obviously, this needs to be at work but also in your personal life with your family, friends and strangers.

It's common sense but is still one of those things that you should always think about on a regular basis and practice it.

Being a contributor is all about adding value to whatever it is that you are doing. Even if you hate your job, you should still go in there and give it your best. At least keep working hard while you're looking for other jobs or other opportunities.

I know that it's easier said than done but as they say, "If it was easy everyone would be doing it." And you know that there are a lot of people out there that hate their jobs so everyone isn't doing it.

If you're doing something you really enjoy, it's a lot easier to be a contributor. In fact, if you enjoy what you're doing, it comes naturally to do your best.

Even if you are retired or unemployed, you should always be contributing. I know that's very hard to do if you are unemployed and you don't have the means. But contributing doesn't necessarily mean giving money. It's more about contributing your time and knowledge than money. Many times money is the last thing somebody needs.

Be a coach or mentor as I mentioned in the previous chapter.

Whether you're an entrepreneur or an employee, it doesn't matter. Probably 99 percent of the people in the world want to be an entrepreneur and start a company that will grow and change the world. I'm not saying that's not possible. Anyone can do it and with the Internet resources available today it's more possible now than ever before. No kidding, the possibilities are endless and your only limitation is yourself.

But that's not for everybody and even if you've sacrificed and tried and failed, don't beat yourself up. It's a learning experience. Move on. Remember the round peg in the square hole thing. Everyone is different and we all have something that we can offer. Whether you're an entrepreneur, self-employed or an employee, go out there and make a difference. Make yourself valuable in your own way.

No matter what category that you fit in, go give it 150 percent of your effort at 200 mph with laser focus and concentration.

Always be contributing in some fashion. Even if you're retired (which is not a good word) go do something. Don't be a couch potato and sit around watching TV. Not that there's anything wrong with watching a little TV. I do it most evenings to wind down. But do it in moderation.

Takeaway:

So no matter what situation comes your way today, think about how you can make a contribution. Even if there's nothing special you think you can contribute, you are wrong. There's always something that you can bring to the table. Just be nice to some stranger at the store or give someone a compliment. That's contributing. That could be more beneficial than you'll ever know. And it will be contagious.

Quotes:

"When you cease to make a contribution, you begin to die."

—Eleanor Roosevelt

LISTEN

Practice being a great listener. Now, I started off by saying "practice" because for 90% of the people out there, this must not be a natural thing. It seems like everyone loves to hear themselves talk, or at least "wants to be heard" might be the more polite way to put it.

Being a good listener is something that I really have to practice. It's not one of my strong suits and does not come naturally for me. My wife Janie gets upset with me for interrupting her in the middle of a story and finishing her sentences. And I know it right away when I do it. I get the look. You know the look. I'm sure that it's because I'm impatient, and that's why I want to finish someone else's story. That's not good. Don't do that and if you do, stop it now. And I'm talking to myself as well. Writing your own book can really teach you something about yourself and this is one of those areas.

Being a good listener is a learned trait for most people. It's another example of where, if you're aware of it, it can be learned. But you have to be aware of it first. If my wife didn't bring it to my attention, I'm not sure I would have realized it. So now I'm very conscious of it when I'm talking to other people. I'm working on being more patient during a conversation.

Remembering a person's name when introduced

People always tell me that they can never remember someone's name after they meet them for the first time. I may not be a good listener naturally but I am very good at this. I learned many years ago that when you're introduced to somebody you should actually listen to what their name is and really hear it. Listening is not the same as hearing. Hear their name when introduced and commit it to memory. Most people are so busy trying to figure out what they're going to say when they are introduced to somebody that they never hear the person's name to begin with. Forget about yourself and what you're going to say. You'll impress someone more if you can remember their name five minutes after you meet them.

Think about that the next time that you're introduced to someone new and really hear them. You can't remember something that you never heard to begin with. So technically you really didn't forget.

Cell phone courtesy

If you can't be a great listener right away at least be a listener of some caliber. I absolutely hate it when I'm talking and someone keeps looking down at their phone. Wow, doesn't that just gripe your ass too? I may have done that myself in the past from time to time, but I do not do that anymore.

If you get a cell phone call (or a text) during a conversation that you absolutely have to take, then excuse yourself and walk away to take care of it quickly. Then come back and apologize because you're not giving that person your full attention.

Don't keep looking down at your phone when someone is talking to you either. When someone does that to me in the middle of a conversation, I just stop talking. I go quiet at that moment. It does get their attention.

While we're on the subject of cell phone etiquette, when you call someone on their cell phone the first thing you should say is "Is this a good time?"

Having cell phones is not like back in the day, when most of us were younger and there were no cell phones. Back then you had to call the person's home phone or office phone. And when they answered the phone they were obviously at home or in their office and probably available to talk.

When you call someone's cell phone now, they could be anywhere, in any situation. That's why I always make sure to ask if it's a good time for them to talk. Now, me on the other hand, I never answer my cell phone if 1) I don't know who it is, and 2) if I can't talk at that time.

I recommend picking and choosing your battles when it comes to your phone conversations. It's about being considerate of everyone's time.

I'd rather someone leave me a voice mail, especially if I don't know what they want and give me a heads up so I can prepare when I call them back. It's about time management and I should not answer the phone if I can't give them my undivided attention.

One more piece of advice when you leave a voice message: Leave a detailed message on what you want. Don't just say "Hey, call me."

Women speak 14,000 words a day (Another funny Alan story)

I have to share another one of my embellished funny stories with you. I'm not sure where I got this info but it's probably on the Internet so it must be true. A woman speaks an average of 14,000 words a day and a man speaks an average of 2,000 words per day. Once I had this information, I could not wait to share it with Janie for no other reason than to joke about this new-found data that I had come across. I'm not saying this to offend either sex, I'm talking about what I read online. Does that mean that men have to be a better listener? I doubt it, but we try.

These facts may actually be true. For example, when Janie asks me how my day went, my responses are pretty short, quick and to the point. When I ask Janie how her day went I get every word, comment and emotion that happened from the time she got up. I'm learning to be a very good listener, or at least good at impersonating a good listener. Jokingly, sometimes I'll tell Janie that her word usage for the day is maxed out. She has reached her 14,000-word limit and she can't borrow from tomorrow's words. (And I'm still alive to write this book.)

You don't have to always be right

Is it important for you to be right all of the time? If that is the case, then you're probably not a good listener. Don't go there. If you catch yourself being this type of person, take a step back and give it some more thought. "Is it really that important for me to be right at this very moment, in this specific conversation?" Especially if the person that you're having a conversation with doesn't appear to be backing down or agreeing with what you're saying. They may be a terrible listener, a negative person, someone that has to always be right or worse yet, all three.

We all know those types of people. I avoid them whenever possible. I'm not saying that to be rude to them. On the contrary, I'm very nice to them. Deep down inside, I take them with a grain of salt and don't get into heated debates and waste my oxygen and time on a no-win situation.

We're the only ones that do it

Years and years ago, we were making a sales call for our engineering business to a new client. I have to admit that sometimes words just fly out of my mouth that I can't get back and sometimes they're just damn funny. Anyway, I was driving the rental car, our client was in the passenger front seat, and my work associate, Jack, was in the back seat. I don't even remember what the question was—I was obviously in marketing mode and trying to impress him—but my response was *"We're the only ones that do it and we do it better than anybody else."* Now, let that statement sink in for a moment.

I didn't even realize what I had said until later that day when Jack could not control his laughter and told me exactly what I had said. That happened over twenty years ago and we still laugh about that today. In fact, we joke about adding it to our marketing material

My point to this is that the client never even heard what I said as far as I know. At least he didn't comment on it. Of course he might still be laughing at me today for all I know. I think he was thinking more about what he was going to say and never heard a word I said. Either way, that is a funny story.

Takeaway:

To wrap this chapter up, be conscious of your listening habits during a conversation and think about how you want someone else's undivided attention when you're talking.

Listening takes patience. And that takes practice. It doesn't come naturally. If you're talking, you can't be listening. This is not a multitasking function. Be sincere, look into a person's eyes and truly listen intently to what they're saying. Don't listen to them talking and think about how to respond. Really hear what they are saying and let it stick to your brain. It's the right thing to do and you'll get much more out of the conversation if you're not selfish with your listening skills.

Quotes:

"Most people do not listen with the intent to understand; they listen with the intent to reply."
—Stephen R. Covey

"Friends are those rare people who ask how we are, and then wait to hear the answer."
—Ed Cunningham

"You cannot truly listen to anyone and do anything else at the same time."
—M. Scott Peck

"We have two ears and one tongue so that we would listen more and talk less."
—Diogenes

YOU GET PAID FOR YOUR VALUE

Everyone gets paid for the value that they bring to the market place. Whether you want to believe it or not, you get paid for exactly what you're worth. I'm sorry to spring that on you, but it's true. That doesn't mean that you can't change that. Just bring more to the table.

If your company pays you $15 per hour and you're willing to accept it, then that's the value. If you don't like it, increase your value. Simple, huh?

I hate it when people say things like "I'm not doing that because they're not paying me enough," or "I'm not working extra hours this week if they're not going to pay me for it." If you want to make yourself more valuable then go the extra mile, give more than is asked of you and help the company or clients make more money. Once you do this, it will give you leverage to renegotiate what they're paying you. You need to prove how valuable you are and then ask for more money. That is more logical than asking for more money now for promising to do better in the future. Add more value first and then request more money.

Another thing some people (the fixed-mindset people) say is "I can't believe that they're paying that CEO five million dollars a year." Well, the truth is that companies normally don't give out money for nothing. It's not a "money-for-nothing-and-the-chicks-are-free" world. That CEO may have brought a billion dollars in profit to the company. Wouldn't you pay someone five million dollars if you could make a billion dollars? I'm just saying. Now, there are some bad examples lately, regarding the big financial firms and Wall Street stuff, but that's not the normal business that I'm talking about here.

It's just like buying a house or anything else. The house is worth what someone is willing to pay for it.

Now, back to my point. If you want to make more money, make yourself more valuable. Go the extra mile. In fact, don't stop there. Go the extra thousand miles. Find out what your client, customer or employer needs, and do more to give it to them.

You'll either get a raise or you'll have no problem making more money somewhere else if your new perceived value is correct.

There are always exceptions to this but normally if someone is getting paid more than they are worth, it is short term situation. And if it isn't, what the hell? Don't dwell on what you don't have control over.

Do the extra things to make yourself more valuable. If you don't know what those things are, make it a point to research and find out. I'm sure that you are already thinking right now of a few ways you can contribute a little more to your company.

Don't do it just one week and expect a raise next month. This is something that you have to do continuously in your mind, over, and over, and over each day, and some day it will come back in return.

Let's pretend that you do this and you don't get it back in compensation. Won't you feel good about doing a better job anyway? If the company or employer screws you over, so be it. They were probably going to screw you over anyway, so get over it and either find another job, or just stay in the job and complain about it. Which one of those sounds like the most fun?

The world does not owe you anything. Appreciate what you have and the opportunities that are available to you today. If you want to make more money then find a way to make yourself more valuable.

Takeaway:

If you want to increase your income, figure out how you can add value to your job or the market place. Once you understand this you will make great progress in advancing your career and income. I promise.

Quotes:

"Don't wish it was easier, wish you were better. Don't wish for less problems, wish for more skills. Don't wish for less challenge, wish for more wisdom."
–Jim Rohn

"You will get all you want in life, if you help enough other people get what they want."
–Zig Ziglar

"Price is what you pay. Value is what you get."
–Warren Buffet

THE CLOCK IS TICKING

We have one life here on Earth as we know it, and it only lasts a very short time in the big scheme of things. We're one little blip on the radar and then we're gone. None of us really know what the big picture is, but no matter what, you better "use it or lose it," as they say.

If you're not being a productive, contributing member to society and serving others, then you're just wasting space and taking oxygen from the rest of us. Now, that might be a harsh statement for a laidback book, but you get my point.

We're here for a short time and I'm sure the big guy has some nice plans for us later on, but for now, we might as well make the best of it while we're here. And while we're at it, we need to make it better for those that will follow us, as our ancestors did for us.

Back to this short life I keep referring to. To put this in perspective, figure out how many days you might have left. Here's an example for me. I could live to 100 or I could die as soon as I finish typing this page but let's look at it somewhere in between. According to life insurance actuarial tables (and I'm sure they're a lot smarter than me) my life span is calculated at 86 years old for white male with my qualities (see how I added qualities?). I'm currently 63, so I have (according to smart people) 23 years remaining. Which is 8,395 days left to live my life. That doesn't sound too bad, but tomorrow when I wake up I'm only going to have 8,394 days remaining. Damn, it's a good thing that I'm writing this book, otherwise I would have been pissed off tomorrow morning because I wasted one of my 8,395 days left. Are you following me on this?

Another way to look at the arithmetic is I have 23 springs, 23 summers, 23 falls and 23 winters left. Wow! I like the 8,395 number better. It feels like a longer time.

DON'T WASTE ONE FRIGGING DAY (or season) depending on how you want to look at it! I'm serious. Enjoy every day like it's going to be your last.

You never know when your calculation is wrong. The 8,395 days that I calculated could easily be zero tomorrow.

Time Wasters

Now that we've established that we have a specific number of days left we have to maximize the quality of that time. Time is our most valuable resource so don't squander it away. It's in limited supply. Make each moment count and above all enjoy it.

Time wasters are around us every day and they can pop up anytime. Sometimes the time wasters are self-induced, based on the decisions that we make. Other times it's outside influences such as circumstances beyond our control or other people. People don't intentionally waste your time but you're in charge of your time so make smart choices when you can. It's easy to let people influence us and steal our time.

We can't always control the people around us from wasting our time but we do have control of our self-induced time wasters. Think about what you spend your time on that does not provide positive results. Positive results might be happiness, having fun, making money, being productive or helping someone else. You have to figure that out for yourself but the point is to think about what you might be wasting your time on that could be better spent doing something else.

Take away:

Enjoy every moment of the time you have left and don't allow time wasters to rob you of it. You can make more money but you can't make more time. Life has an expiration date.

I'm really glad that I'm writing this book. It has opened my own eyes. Even though I have truly believed what I'm writing about in this chapter, I have not fully lived and taken actions like I should have. That is stopping today. You can't get back time. Once today is over, it's over and tomorrow may not come. Starting today, I'm going to start on my bucket list. Let's rock this place.

Quotes:

"This is not a dress rehearsal, this is your life."
—Bill Murray

"Life is too short. Grudges are a waste of perfect happiness. Laugh when you can. Apologize when you should and let go of what you can't change."
—Anonymous

"Waste your money and you're only out of money, but waste your time and you've lost a part of your life."
—Michael Leboeuf

"Live every day as if it were going to be your last; for one day you're sure to be right."
—Harry Morant

LIVE UNTIL YOU DIE

The last chapter talked about how much time or how little time we might have left on this Earth. Now that I have your attention on the amount of time remaining let's talk about what how you spend that time. What you do with that time is up to you but do whatever it takes to make sure it is quality time that you enjoy. Use the time efficiently and don't waste it on things that you don't enjoy. Go out there and live until your countdown ends. Don't just exist, really live it.

Always, always, always be growing, learning and teaching until the end. If you are not living, you are dying. You can rest when you die.

I'm not saying to never rest. That's unrealistic. We all need to take time to relax and recharge our batteries. It is mandatory requirement in order to maintain a high level of productivity when we are working. Plus, we work hard so that we can reap the rewards when the time is right.

When you accomplish one of your goals, go out and party like it's your birthday. Rock and roll brothers and sisters. Here I go getting crazy again. Seriously, reward yourself when you reach a goal. If it was a big goal, then give yourself a big reward. It it's a small goal give yourself a small reward. Only you can be the judge of that. Either way, reward yourself. The reward, no matter how small, reinforces why you're doing something in the first place and will keep you motivated.

Someone once said, "Everything is good in moderation." This is probably a smart philosophy for some things. I realize this might sound contrary to my statement "If it's worth doing, it's worth overdoing," but we all have our own speed limit. You just have to figure out yours. It's your life so live it in your laidback way at your speed.

Let's get back to this moderation subject. I'm not really the person to speak about moderation since I tend to "overdo" stuff. But that is changing for me since I started writing this book. I am learning the value of slowing down a bit, looking at the stars, smelling the roses and appreciating the life I have.

Actually, I've always appreciated what I have but I have not always smelled the things that I should have smelled.

Since starting this book, I try take a 15-minute break in the morning and in the afternoon. I close my office door, sit in my chair and do nothing but listen to myself breathe for 15 minutes. That's all I got on that story. I don't have any deep transcendental meditation tips or anything like that. It's me sitting in a chair doing nothing. And sitting anywhere for 15 minutes doing nothing is a whole new concept for me.

Retirement

I'm at that age where a lot of my friends are retired or getting ready to retire. I also have a lot of friends and associates that are older than me that have no intention of retiring. Bob Proctor is a great example of this. He's a fantastic teacher and motivator. He's been speaking, coaching and mentoring for 60 years. He's over 80 years old and is going stronger than ever. This type of person inspires me and there are more people out there in the world like this than you think. What that says to me is that I can do what I'm doing now for another 20 years or longer.

Even though most of these people could retire financially, they have no desire to quit. What I have realized is that your desire to retire or not, is directly proportional to how much you enjoy what you do.

Since I'm getting close to that so-called retirement age, everyone asks me when I'm going to retire. My answer is "I'm not". I don't like the word "retire." It sounds so final. I'm not saying never quit your day job or that career that you may have had for 40 years. If that's what you've worked and planned for all of these years that's great. Congratulations!

The formal definition of *retire* is "to leave one's job and cease to work." Wow. Cease to work. Just the word "cease" doesn't sound appealing to me but this is my take on the retirement subject.

Everyone has their own definition of retired. I came up with the definition of laidback and it's not even a word. Come up with your own definition of "retired" and go do it.

Most people look forward to retirement and plan on it their whole life. I'm all about planning for it financially, but that's not what I'm talking about here. Even if you are financially set, stay productive and do what you enjoy.

I'm not saying to work your ass off and die with regrets of not having time to enjoy life. I'm stating the contrary. Do what you enjoy, work hard at it and don't cheat yourself out of doing the things that really matter to you.

Make a bucket list

Writing this book was on my bucket list and here I am writing this book.

Another thing on my immediate bucket list is to get electric drums. I've wanted a drum set my entire life but just never got around to it. Now, you can have an electric drum set, put your headphones on, play like you're a rock star and nobody can hear how bad you are.

My second bucket list item is to be able to go to Florida or somewhere warm more often and for longer periods in the winter. I don't want to be cold anymore. Life is too short to sit around the house while it's cold and gray outside for one third of the year. That's about 120 days a year, if it's a short winter in Ohio. That's 3,120 days of my theoretical time remaining. This does not mean that I'm going to retire. It means that I have to get creative and figure out how to work remotely outside of the office.

As my dad used to say, "We're all here because we're not all there." He thought he was funny too. He's the one that also said, "Let's have a few cocktails before dinner. I don't like to eat on an empty stomach." I don't know how this relates to the live-until-you-die subject, but it came across my mind so I threw in some humor to see if you're actually paying attention.

Takeaway:

Don't just exist each day that you have left. Maximize the quality of that time and experience as much as possible. Wake up each morning with an awesome attitude and learn something new every day. Each time you learn something new, it's one more thing that you can pass on to others. Leave a positive mark on everyone that you come in contact with. Make a bucket list and mark each item off when you accomplish it. If you complete your bucket list, go celebrate and make another list.

Don't just survive. Do whatever you need to do to live each day to the fullest, enjoy the shit out of it and make an impact.

Quotes:

"Dream as if you'll live forever and live as if you'll die today."

—James Dean

"Strength and growth come only through continuous effort and struggle."

—Napoleon Hill

"Intellectual growth should commence at birth and cease only at death."

—Albert Einstein

IT's YOUR FUNERAL

How many times have you been told "It's your funeral"? Let's pretend that it is. I know, it's another morbid line of thinking, but we'll put a little lighter spin on it since I've been preaching positivity throughout the book.

Plan ahead

When my mom passed away, she had it all planned out. She had the funeral paid for, the casket picked out and everything handled. This made it easy on everyone in the family. My mom even wrote her own obituary for me to edit as I wanted when it came time for that. Of course, I added a lot to it since she was a very humble person and she was always about everyone else.

Granted, when she planned it out she was almost 70 years old and it was during the time that her husband had passed away. That does give you a wakeup call. My mom was very organized and I'm sure that's how I got to be this way as well.

If you're 20, 30 or 40 years old, you're probably not going to gravitate to this chapter as well as the older crew, but hopefully you'll keep this in mind as time goes on. It's another one of those "don't procrastinate" moments. Once you get this all done and planned out you won't have to think about it anymore.

Leave a mark

I saw a video not too long ago with Bob Goff being interviewed. Bob wrote the very popular book *Love Does*. He is a very funny guy with a great attitude. Watch his YouTube videos and you'll get another great viewpoint on a laidback life mindset.

Bob Goff said that if you think about it, nobody knew or ever heard of you a hundred years ago. Duh! Obviously, since I wasn't born yet. But then he said that in the next 100 years nobody is going to know who you are either. Yes, your grandkids may know you now and maybe your great grand kids but what about your great-great-great-great-grandkids? Sure, they might get on ancestry.com or something like that and find out what your name was, who you married, and how that relates to them in the family tree, but they won't really know you. But Goff said now that he's written his books, those grandchildren and whoever is interested will be able to read something that he left behind and get a glimpse of who he was.

I watched this about a month after I started writing my book. What a great revelation. I was moving kind of slow on my book, but after watching that, I got motivated to finish this book. Even if my book isn't perfect, I'm going to get the damn thing done. I can always edit it or change it later, but I better get this sucker done in case I don't have as many days as the smart insurance people have calculated.

Takeaway:

Leave a mark and make a difference. This book is like my obituary except I would prefer to think of it as a little glimpse into the shit that goes through my simple mind. How's that sound? That is more like something that a laidback person would say. Don't you think?

Quotes:

"I'm always relieved when someone is delivering a eulogy and I realize I'm listening to it."
—George Carlin

"It's not that I'm afraid to die. I just don't want to be there when it happens."
—Woody Allen

"We make a living by what we get; we make a life by what we give."
—Winston Churchill

DON'T WORRY ABOUT
WHAT OTHERS THINK

D on't worry about what others think. This is more important to abide by than people realize if you want to grow. It's not easy to do but it's something that has to be considered.

It's important to have a great self-image and there's no better way to have that than with confirmation from others. Everybody needs support from others, and constructive criticism is very important. You can't just have friends that tell you how great you are all of the time just to be nice. You need to know the truth if you're open to improving, and willing to listen.

Your close friends' and families opinions are important, but that's not what I'm referring to in this chapter. I'm referring to people that don't even know you or at the very least, don't have your best interest in mind. If it's a close friend or family member that you truly trust, then sometimes it does matter what they think. But even then, sometimes friends and family can hold you back from your dreams.

If you're doing it for the wrong reasons or you worry about what the neighbors think, get that thinking out of your mind. Just ignore it. Maybe ignore is not the right word but don't let that affect the decisions you make and the actions you take.

A lot of people don't take the leap of faith or and make intelligent decisions because they're afraid what somebody else might think. Or they worry about what people will think if they fail.

Imagine what someone could accomplish if they were not afraid of what someone else thinks. Everybody has their own risk-tolerance level, but each time you step outside the box, the box gets a little bigger.

Most people never really do what they want to do in life because they are worried about what other people might think. If you really take a look at this statement and let it sink in, then you'll realize how crazy that is.

What makes that even worse is that "people" (whoever we're referring to here) probably aren't really thinking about you as much as you think they are. There's another reason not to worry about what they think. The truth is that those "other people" are probably too busy thinking about themselves and maybe worried about what you think of them. Did you ever think of that?

I'm not saying this is all bad, it's just human nature. Everybody has their own inner world. They're in their world and you're in your world. I'm not saying that everyone is self centered, but they are in a sense.

Don't do something crazy like letting others (friends, family, and especially people that you don't even know that well) control your life and hold you back. Be yourself and go get whatever it is you want out of life. Don't cheat yourself out of living your life because you're worried about cheating someone else out of what they think of you.

If they really do think about you, they are going to have an opinion of you so just accept it. The real issue is how you react to it. A tiger doesn't lose sleep over what sheep think.

One of my common Al-isms is "THAT'S BULLSHIT." I realize that those words by themselves are not original, but you should hear the tone when I say it. It's funnier when I say it and now that I typed it out, it's really not that funny. But this is a good chapter to say it. If you're living life on someone else's terms or what they think of you, then my response is "THAT'S BULLSHIT." Think about those two words whenever you find yourself worrying about what someone else thinks about you.

Don't let someone else rent space in your head without your permission.

Takeaway:

Go be yourself and live life on your terms no matter what other people think. Remember, they are probably not thinking about you as much as you think they are and if they are "Who gives a rat's ass what they think?" Don't let these misguided thoughts keep you from accomplishing your dreams.

Be confident, be you, jump outside the box and don't let anyone hold you back. **Dance like nobody is watching.**

Quotes:

"I'm sorry, if you were right, I'd agree with you."
—Robin Williams

"We are so scared of being judged that we look for every excuse to procrastinate."
—Erica Jong

"Just keep moving forward and don't give a shit about what anybody thinks. Do what you have to do, for you."
—Johnny Depp

"Just a reminder, what other people think of you is none of your business."
—Regina Brett

IF YOU FAIL TO PLAN,
YOU PLAN TO FAIL

To quote Benjamin Franklin, "If you fail to plan, you are planning to fail." I'm pretty sure that old Ben Franklin knew a thing or two. That saying is one of my common quotes that my friends hear me say all the time. In fact, they're probably tired of me saying it. It's another one of my Al-isms. You'll also notice that I think I'm pretty funny. I don't know if my friends agree with that, but at least I tend to be entertained by my own self-proclaimed funniness.

I don't have a big chapter about this but I had to get it out there since it is one of the things I say all the time. I am a planner, and some people, including my wife, call me "Anal Al" because I'm all about being organized, making a plan, setting a schedule and keeping a task list. That's OK. That's the way I am and it works for me for my laidback lifestyle.

Take baby steps in planning

If you're not an Anal Al type, start by jotting things down, even if it's a small to do list on a calendar. There are a lot of programs and apps available to make it simple and efficient. Don't over complicate it. I'm a big fan of using the phone and computer apps but I'm a bigger fan of keeping it simple.

You don't have to have detailed project management schedule. This is the engineer coming out now. Jot things down, and set up a plan to get you where you want to go one step at a time. Don't stress out about it. Keep it simple and come up with what works for you.

A straight line is more efficient than zigzagging all the way to the goal line. Even if you just have a few steps mapped out, a few zigs is better than a lot of zags. A small plan is better than no plan.

The more specific you are at defining your goals, the more laser-focused and efficient you can be in hitting that target.

It is impossible to avoid failure so plan on it. You have to fail before you can succeed. It's a matter of how many failures that it takes and how you react to the failures. If the statistics indicate that you have to talk to ten people to get one customer, then go talk to the first nine as quick possible. You know you're going to fail so you might as well just jump in and do it quickly. Fail fast and fail forward.

Don't get into the paralysis of analysis mode. Some people evaluate the shit out of making a move, and never do it. Others jump as many times as it takes, make the mistakes quickly and then start over with their new-found information. More times than not those people try, fail and succeed before the others start.

Do not wait until everything is perfect before you start. It will never happen.

Learn from your mistakes

Learn from your mistakes, and don't make the same mistakes over and over and expect different outcomes.

A good example of this is me. Back in the '80s I was young and bulletproof. I studied every possible real estate investing course available and thought I knew it all. I proceeded to buy rental houses. I found out very quickly that I sucked at managing the properties and many of the day-to-day details. I made every mistake possible and fell on my face.

Fast-forward 30 years. I jumped back into the real estate investing business eight years ago and it's going stronger than I ever imagined.

When I got back into it for the second time, I was asked many times by my friends, "Why in the world would you ever want to do that again based on the outcome before?" My response was "It would be crazy not to."

Knowing this can be a very successful business if done correctly, I had to do it again. After all, if a person learns from their mistakes then I probably got an equivalent of a full blown college education back then. This time it worked out. I'm doing everything the exact opposite that I did the first time.

Granted, I am treading more carefully as I get older and wiser. I realize now that I'm not bulletproof. But if I had not gone out on a limb and made all of those mistakes 30 years ago I would not be where I am today.

Be careful out there, but don't be so careful that you never reach out of your comfort zone and do nothing.

If you don't fail then you're not trying hard enough. Fail forward, fail fast and don't waste the failures. Use them to succeed.

Success is many times up to the eye of the beholder as well. Even if you don't succeed reaching your goal you still gave it a shot. You were successful in going after it no matter the outcome. Don't beat yourself up.

Takeaway:

Plan as much as possible to minimize failures, but accept the failures as a lesson learned and one step closer to success. Your odds are better for success if you have a plan but don't wait until everything is perfect before you start either.

Success doesn't happen by accident. Increase your odds by having a plan no matter how small the plan.

Quotes:

"I have not failed. I've just found 10,000 ways that won't work."
—Thomas Edison

"Success is not final, failure is not fatal: it is the courage to continue that counts."
—Winston Churchill

"My attitude has always been, if you fall flat on your face, at least you're moving forward. All you have to do is get back up and try again."
—Richard Branson

"I used to be afraid of failing at something that really mattered to me, but now I'm more afraid of succeeding at things that don't matter."
—Bob Goff

What Are You Waiting For?

Hello! McFly! What are you waiting for?

This chapter is about procrastination. Avoid it at all cost. Seriously. If you're a procrastinator then you should take some simple steps to change that. This is easy for me to say because I am definitely not a procrastinator. I'm not sure if I was like this as a kid, but if I was, I've outgrown it. I'm the opposite of procrastination.

The opposite of procrastination

I did look up the opposite of procrastinate and I did not get the answer I was looking for. It said "anxious" or something like that. I was looking for a more positive word than just "anxiousness" so I could put it in this book. Since I came up with my own definition of the word "laidback" I'm going to do it here as well. The opposite of procrastination is "to get the shit done now." Or let's be a little more politically correct and call it "productive."

When things are left undone

Procrastination never did anything for me, except cause me to worry constantly about what I have on my to-do list that I haven't completed yet. It easily spirals out of control once you get this procrastination thing going. It's the same thing that I said in a previous chapter about multi-tasking. Remember the routine about "finishing task A before starting task B" and so forth? If you don't finish A before B, you'll be stressing about A and not get either one of them done with much focus.

If you have something on your plate that you can get done now, then by all means get it out of the way and off of your mind. Don't keep your mind cluttered with stuff that could have been completed yesterday.

Clean your plate regularly. Don't eat on a dirty plate.

Moving too fast will teach you more than moving too slow

By not being a procrastinator, I have been guilty of taking action too quickly based on stupid decisions, but that shit happens sometimes. All of that is hindsight now. There are multiple times where I've jumped, taken action, and made bonehead mistakes before other people got out of their chair. I'm pretty sure I learned more than they did, and positive that I've lived life a little more than they did in that same time frame.

If you do something fast and make a mistake, at least you learned something quickly. Then you can go do it again with more experience.

Take action and move forward. The problem is not going to disappear. In many instances, it will probably be worse if you wait. If you put it off, it will be cluttering up your mind. If not consciously, it will subconsciously mess with your head. Pick away at your "To Do" list, fast and furious. Clean the slate so you can move on to the next productive task.

Takeaway:

Don't get stuck painfully agonizing over every little decision. Get out of the paralysis of analysis mode and just do it. Make a decision and go after it. As us golfers say, "Put the frigging ball on the ground and tee it off."

Quotes:

"When there is a hill to climb don't think that by waiting will make it smaller."
—Anonymous

"Don't procrastinate. Putting off an unpleasant task until tomorrow simply gives you more time for your imagination to make a mountain out a possible molehill. More time for anxiety to sap your self-confidence. Do it now, brother, do it now."
—Author Unknown

"Procrastination is like a credit card: it's a lot of fun until you get the bill."
—Christopher Parker

"Begin while others are procrastinating. Work while others are wishing."
—William Arthur Ward

DON'T BE ART

Art is my imaginary twin brother, or you might say, my evil alter ego. He's an asshole.

The story behind my pretend brother: Art all started a few years back when we were golfing. I golf with a group of guys each week, and we're always joking around. That's what we do. Golf, drink beer and joke around. Most of the jokes are embellishments of our own lives and actions. I love embellishing on real life stuff that I've done for the sake of a joke.

One day I was telling the guys a story about my first job out of college for an engineering firm. I worked really hard and enjoyed it. It was exciting and I was really good at what I did. At least I thought I was making an impact, and thought the boss was noticing my excellent work.

After several months at the job, my boss called me into his office. He was a really old guy. Actually he was probably about the same age as I am now, but back then I thought he was ancient. When he called me into his office I thought he was going to tell me how good of job I was doing. I wasn't wrong. He did tell me that I was doing a great job but his exact words were, "You're doing a great job, Art." Hello! My name is Alan. OK, so I'm not sure he wasn't a little off in the head, but he was an engineer and doing engineering stuff so he shouldn't have been too senile. Either way, that's how Art was born.

Now let's get back to how it relates to my life now and golf.

Golf is a crazy game and if you're a golfer you can relate to this. For example, you can play ten rounds of golf and out of those ten, you might have a few really good rounds but mostly average rounds. Then one day, all of a sudden out of nowhere, you can really suck. You can't figure out why. Sometimes your golf game can be as different as night and day from one day to the next.

On those days that you suck, it's like another person is playing the game. When I do that, I blame Art.

That son-of-a-bitch snuck out here on the golf course again and took my place. Now, that is pretty funny.

After I told my Art story from forty years ago, we carried that train of thought over to our golf game as a joke. When you play bad that day, it has to be your imaginary, red-neck, alter ego twin brother playing. I named mine Art. We have some big laughs about it. Everyone has an Art in their life, whether they want to admit it or not. The big key is to keep Art at home and don't bring him out in public.

It's been a few years now since Art came onto the scene in my golfing circles and the story line is still going strong. In fact, it's getting stronger every year. We always come up with new ways to embellish and laugh about Art every day. We go on and on each time we play golf and embellish on made up stories about what Art has done or would have done if he was real.

Now when we come in after a round of golf, the big joke is "Hey, Big Al, did you play today or did Art play?" If I played well, then Big Al played. If I sucked at golf that day then Art (my evil nemesis) was the culprit. I try to leave Art at home chained to a radiator in the basement but he still keeps getting free and showing up at the course at the most inappropriate times. He's embarrassing to be around.

We've had so much fun laughing about Art, that all of my buddies now have their own alter egos. Greg Keller's evil twin is Gary. Dana Schultz' is Darrell. Jeff Matola's is Jerry and Jdub's is Jake. Whenever we play with a new person or someone that doesn't have an alter ego name, we have one for him by the end of the round. So the Arts, Garys, Darrells, Jerrys and Jakes of the world are multiplying every day. But Art will always be at the top of the charts in that fraternity.

If you didn't notice your alter ego name starts with the same letter as your real name. If your alter ego (or stupid side of you) does not have a name yet then give it a name. At least then you can put a name to the person that is holding you back and you'll have a better understanding of how to deal with them when they show up.

That's the story of how Art came to be. Even though it's a joke, the point of the story is "Don't be that guy." Sometimes you can't help it but be aware of it. Every now and then you have an Art come out and do some stupid stuff. It's kind of like have a little angel on one shoulder, and a devil on the other. Art is the devil. We all have one somewhere. We all make mistakes and we all make stupid decisions now and then, but that's OK. Just make sure that Art is not in control. You are in control. Put him in his place. You can listen to him now and then but just laugh at him, joke about it and then go back and be your true self.

There's another, more serious, YouTube video with the same theme. It's done by Patrick David Betts on his YouTube channel. It's not only entertaining but it addresses the open-minded entrepreneur versus the closed minded type of mentality. I recommend watching it. It's only a few minutes long and it's excellent for "attitude awareness."

Takeaway:

"Don't be an asshole." This should be an easy chapter to remember, don't you think? Nobody thinks that they're an asshole. They always think that the other person is the asshole. Think about it in depth to make sure that you're not Art in disguise.

Quotes:

I could only find two good quotes from famous people that I like relating to this chapter.

"You're not wrong, Walter. You're just an asshole."
—The Dude, *The Big Lebowski*

"Don't be Art."
—Alan McComas

All Winners Are Sandbaggers.

When I say all winners are sandbaggers, I am being sarcastic. I'm referring to the attitude of bad losers.

Let me back up a second and explain what I'm talking about. I'm an avid golfer so I like to look at life's lessons through golf.

Golf is a wonderful game and it teaches a person life lessons. If you really want to get to know someone, go spend four hours with them in a round of golf. You'll figure out pretty quickly what type of person they are.

Everyone has a handicap in golf. The handicap is based on your best ten out of your last twenty scores. If you're honest when you post your scores, you would have an accurate handicap. A sandbagger is someone that posts higher scores than they actually shoot, so they get a higher handicap in tournaments, which gives them an advantage when the money is on the table. I personally don't think anyone I know does this, but I am a trusting soul.

Where I'm going with this is, that after a tournament, there's always someone at the losers' table that complains that the winners have to be sandbagging. Maybe sometimes they are, but the point I'm trying to make is that it doesn't matter.

If someone is sandbagging that's their problem. You can't do anything about it except bitch to all of your friends and they don't want to hear it.

It's usually the same people complaining about the sandbaggers who are complaining about the government, or service in a restaurant, or whatever. It's always going to be something. Don't be that person. Let it go. It's a loser mentality. Don't think like a loser and blame others.

Theoretically, if everyone's handicap is accurate (and that might be a pipe dream) then everyone has the same chance of winning. If you play better than your handicap that day, then you'll have a good chance of winning. It's not easy to beat your handicap, since the formula is based on your best scores and not on your average score. Just strive to beat your handicap, and don't worry about other peoples. Another point to make is that if you beat your handicap more times than not, then your handicap will go down and there you are. It's a vicious cycle, but it is how you improve. It's funny how that works. See how all of this golf stuff relates to life?

Takeaway:

Go adopt a winning attitude. Look for the opportunities in every problem. Don't blame others or circumstances for what has gone wrong. Stay positive and congratulate others when they win or succeed. Don't begrudge people that seem to have beat you, or succeeded more than you. Go out there the next time and give it your best. Being nice and a good sport trumps all else. Kick their ass the next time.

Quotes:

"Winners focus on winning. Losers focus on winners."
—Anonymous

LAUGH

I am the funniest person I know. At least, that's what the little voice in my head tells me and that's the only one that matters (other than my wife). See how funny I can be? If you want to be laidback, laugh, laugh a lot and laugh at yourself.

Don't take yourself so serious. There are others that have laughed at you in the past, whether you want to admit it or not. You might as well join their party and have fun with it.

I'm very good at this and quite frankly have a knack for it. In fact, I crack myself up all the time with my own stupid actions and jokes.

I also embellish on true stories and events to make the truth even funnier. Sometimes they aren't funny stories at all, but when I'm done, they're a full comedy series in the making. I suggest you try it as well.

If you decide to make some changes after reading this book do it with a sense of humor. You can't change everything all at once, but if you can laugh at yourself, the whole process will be much more enjoyable. If you don't make it enjoyable you won't do it. Make it easy on yourself.

I realize that everyone can't be smiling and laughing all of the time, but I'm sure you will agree that laughter is fun and it's contagious. If you find yourself a little down and out, and need a good laugh I have a quick solution. I want you to do it right now so you don't forget about it later. It's that important. Are you ready for my secret trick to get you to laugh?

An exercise to get you to laugh in 3 minutes

Go to YouTube and search for any video of someone laughing uncontrollably. You can't help but laugh when you hear or see people laughing uncontrollably. I just did it and came up with "Can't stop laughing moments on TV." And within two minutes I just about peed my pants laughing. I'm still wiping the tears away. It was a great break from writing and it's a good exercise to do now and then.

Go do this exercise right now and try to come back to this book without a smile. You can't do it. I dare you. Your stomach will hurt and you will have tears in your eyes from laughing.

Takeaway

I hope you did the exercise and enjoyed it. So far that's been my favorite thing in this book. I'm positive that I'm getting more out of writing this book than anyone reading it.

Laugh a lot, laugh at yourself, don't take yourself too seriously and make others laugh. There's nothing more fulfilling than to know that you put a smile on someone's face especially if it brought them out of a funk.

Laughing is contagious. Spread it around.

Quotes:

"It's your outlook on life that counts. If you take yourself lightly and don't take yourself too seriously, pretty soon you can find the humor in our everyday lives. And sometimes it can be a lifesaver."
—Betty White

"Surround yourself with people who take their work seriously, but not themselves, those who work hard and play hard."
—Colin Powell

"Enjoy the little things, for one day you may look back and realize they were the big things."
—Robert Brault

"Do not take life too seriously. You will never get out of it alive."
—Elbert Hubbard

CLOSING SUMMARY

I hope you enjoyed the book as much as I enjoyed writing it. And I hope you got as much out of it as I did. I thought this would be my first and only book but now my little brain is full of additional topics that I want to share. So now I'm going to start my next book.

If you do nothing else with my tips in this book, just be yourself. No matter what, be true to yourself and enjoy every step of the way through life.

Janie has these little signs around our house and the one in our bathroom is appropriate for this closing chapter. "Happiness is wanting what you have."

Don't try to be someone else. It's too much work and people know it right away. Don't fake it 'til you make it as some would preach. There's only one of you, so go and do it your way.

Study and learn from others, but take that information and go do it your way. Just use the information from others as tools in your toolbox.

If you enjoy personal development and motivational books like I do, I hope this book added a little value to your life.

If you have not been interested in personal development materials in the past, I hope this book sparked your interest. There are many books, audios podcasts and websites available today that can change your life. I've included a list of my recommendations at the end of this book if you're interested.

It helps to read a little bit every day. Even if it's just a few pages and even if you've read them many times before. You only remember about 2 to 3 percent of what you read. It helps to go back and read things multiple times.

I recommend going back through my book and highlighting the items that you think will help you the most.

Then go back and read this book again in a few months. I do it all of the time with these books. It reinforces and rejuvenates the attitude and mindset.

It's a lifetime of work in progress, and is something that needs to be studied and practiced every day. It's no different than your car. Your attitude and mindset need an ongoing maintenance program.

If you're not a reader, like I am, go get the audio versions and listen to them in your car. Time spent driving is normally wasted or somewhat unproductive. Plus, it's a good uninterrupted alone time that allows you to think about what you're listening to. Don't take notes while you're driving. Take this from my personal experience.

Takeaway:

Go Out there and start living a laidback lifestyle. Make opportunities out of problems. Create success from failures. You're going to have problems and failures so the only thing you have control over is how you react to them and what you do about it.

Don't try to be someone else. You are who you are. Do the best that you can and enjoy it. There's always someone worse off than you, so count your blessings.

Be kind to others, go forward with an open mind and don't judge others.

Appreciate what you have and your life. As I said at the beginning of the book, you may already have a Laidback Life but you just don't realize it yet.

Be Cool, Peace out and Stay Laidback.

Quotes:

"People often say that motivation doesn't last. Well, neither does bathing - that's why we recommend it daily."
—Zig Ziglar

"Later dudes! Let 'er rip, hang ten!"
—Clark Griswold, *National Lampoon's Christmas Vacation*

Dedication Chapter to My Mom

What Would Patsy Do?

This book is dedicated to my mom, Patsy Brown. She made me who I am today. She was a single mom with very modest means. She worked hard and raised me and my brother Pat with the help of her parents, my grandparents, Ma and Pa.

I spoke at my mom's funeral last year and the words were very easy. She always seemed to do the right thing, had a positive attitude, treated everyone the same and was never judgmental. And 50 years ago there was a lot of prejudice and judgmental people. There weren't as many open minded people back then, which really says a lot about my mom. She was ahead of the times when it comes to that area. I didn't realize it back then but I sure do now.

I never really got into trouble, but did have a little incident in college regarding some pot in my dorm. Oops! How did that stuff get there? Anyway, I don't need to go into details on that, but the point is that I had to go to my mom about this situation. I hated doing that for the obvious reasons but mainly because I didn't want to hurt or disappoint her. But I had no choice since I needed money and advice for legal purposes.

I went home for the weekend and asked my mom to sit down and I told her the story. This was the early '70s and she was never around pot other than what was on the news. Plus, I had no prior problems, so she never would have suspected me to be involved with anything like this. I won't expand on the details but my point is this was all new stuff and I thought I was going to really drop a bombshell on her. It was devastating for me to stand there and tell her what happened.

When I got done with the story she never batted an eye. She looked at me, and obviously could see my stress level and how worried I was and she said, "OK, what can I do to help you get through this?" I don't remember the exact words but it was something like that. She was great.

She was like this my whole life. She never over reacted, handled everything with a calm attitude and just got shit done. So when I got done writing the eulogy there was one sentence that summed it all up. "What would Patsy do?"

Here's the actual eulogy that I gave at her funeral last year.

> I just want to say that our mom was the best mom that anyone could have asked for. I know everyone says that, but this is really true.
>
> She's responsible for every fiber of my being, and not just physically, but how I look at life and treat others.
>
> She always took care of others before herself. She was a care giver.
>
> She never said a bad thing about anyone.
>
> She was always open-minded and saw the good in everyone. She was open minded on many issues before it was even cool to be open-minded on certain topics. She never did anything just to be cool. She did things because they were the right thing to do.

She never got upset with us. Even when we got in trouble (which wasn't too often, just a couple issues for me and Pat just out of high school) she never got mad. She always said "OK, let's figure this out and see what we need to do to get through it." She was always positive and a problem solver. She was never judgmental.

Mom raised me and Pat on a very modest income and worked her butt off for us. She sacrificed a lot for us, but knowing her, she wouldn't have had it any other way. You don't realize this stuff until later in life.

After raising us, she then took care of her parents, Ma and Pa, and Aunt Noke. After Pa died, she married Jim Brown "Hunk" and looking back, this was the best thing that ever happened to both of them.

They had a great life and really took care of each other. I could not have asked for a better situation than her marrying Hunk. They were really good for each other and I want to thank Hunk for everything he did for our family.

I'm sure they're up there in Heaven together right now, sitting in their Lazy Boy chairs and watching

Bonanza or John Wayne movies together. And I'm sure the TV is really loud.

And in between commercials, she's probably taking care of Ma and Pa and Aunt Noke. It gives me great peace knowing they're all together now and none of them are suffering.

The past few years have been really tough, and it's really not been my mom since the Alzheimer's got bad, but she never suffered physically, and still never complained. She was so nice to all her caretakers, no matter how she felt. And every one of her caretakers loved her. She was always joking around with them and they've shared their memories this week with us as well.

I do want to thank Hospice for such great work. We've had our share of Hospice experiences lately, between Pat Boggs and Sharry Justice, and we really appreciate their help. Most of us think of hospice as the last few days of your life, which is the case for most people, but we learned that's not everything. My mom has been under the watchful eye of Hospice for almost two years. It's not that she received constant care from them. They stopped in a couple times a week and helped out the assisted living facility with showers and feeding, and stuff like that, but the most important thing they did was call me at least once a week just to let me know the facility was doing a good job. That was a huge relief since you don't know what's happening when you're not there, and I already felt guilty enough because I wasn't there more often. So I just wanted to recognize and thank Hospice for everything they did. It's hard for people to realize how much help they give until you need it.

I knew this was a sad time for all of us, but we need to keep in mind that Mom lived a full and happy life with no regrets, and she's not suffering anymore. She did what made her happy her whole life and that was taking care of people. We really do need to celebrate her life, and when any of you get in a bind or get upset about something, just sit back and think "What would Patsy do? How would she react?" That would make her smile each time each of you did that, the next time you're in a bind.

I just want to say, I love you Mom and thank you from the bottom of my heart for a great life and taking care of al of us. You've always been our rock, and an inspiration to me and how I live my life, and I know you made a difference on the rest of the family and everyone you have touched.

You've suffered enough the past couple of years, and you can rest now. I'll try to handle things down here like you would have done. I'm not going to say goodbye, Mom. Just get some rest and I'll see you later.

ABOUT THE AUTHOR

Alan McComas is Vice President of SEI Engineers in Powell, OH. Alan has been with the firm since its beginning in 1984. In addition to Alan's career at SEI, he is a part time entrepreneur.

From his home (and part-time), Alan started his real estate investing business in 2009. He buys and rehabs single family homes.

When Alan is not at the office at SEI he is either working on his part-time real estate investing business, listening to personal development audios, writing books or playing golf. And not always in that order. He really likes to golf so sometimes he squeezes that in before some of his other tasks.

Alan is known by everyone around him for his problem-solving skills and his great sense of humor.

He's just damn funny, easy to get along with and enjoyable to be around.

He is committed to helping others by sharing his thoughts and insights about all aspects of life, based on his personal and professional experiences.

Alan and Janie also have a networking marketing business, providing home and business services, and Janie manages the real estate investing business from their home office.

Alan and Janie are all about helping others and contributing to charitable organizations. Janie is involved in the local hospice community and sits on the local hospice board.

Janie hosts the "Big Al Charity Golf Outing" each year to benefit local charities.

RECOMMENDATIONS

Alan's recommendations for more Self Development

Books, Websites and Podcasts

Lessons of a Life by Jim Rohn

Mini Habits by Stephen Guise

Live the Life You Have Always Dreamed Of! by Chris Widener

The Compound Effect by Darren Hardy

The Virgin Way by Richard Branson

Mindsets: The New Psychology of Success by Carol S. Dweck.

7 Habits of Highly Effective People by Stephen Covey

Declutter Your Mind by S.J. Scott and Barrie Davenport

No Limits by John C. Maxwell

Master Your Time, Master Your Life by Brian Tracy

Just Shut Up and Do It by Brian Tracy

Live Your Dreams by Les Brown

Reinvent Yourself by James Altucher

Doing the Impossible by Patrick Bet David

You Were Born Rich by Bob Proctor

The Power of Positive Thinking by Norman Vincent Peale

Made in the USA
Lexington, KY
12 April 2019